NITYA SUTRAS

The Revelations of Nityananda
from the Chidakash Gita

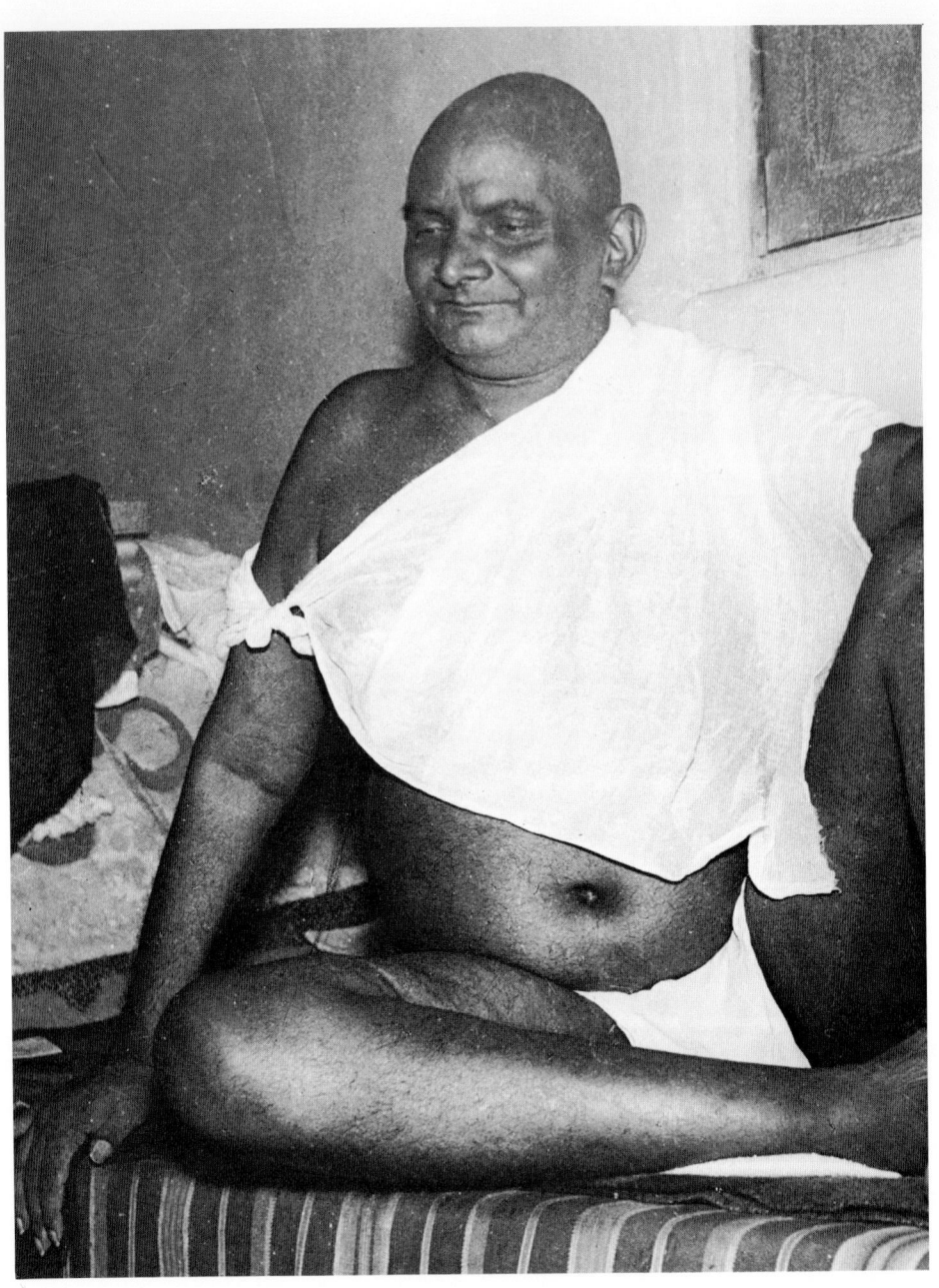

Bhagavan Nityananda

NITYA SUTRAS

The Revelations of Nityananda
from the Chidakash Gita

M.U. Hatengdi
and
Swami Chetanananda

RUDRA PRESS · Cambridge, Massachusetts

RUDRA PRESS
P.O. Box 1973
Cambridge, Massachusetts 02238

© 1985 M.U. Hatengdi and Swami Chetanananda

Cover painting: Wendell Field
Photographs: M.D. Suvarna

All rights reserved. No part of this book may be reproduced in any form or by any means, without permission in writing from the publisher.

Manufactured in the United States of America.

First Edition

ISBN 0–915801-02–7

To all disciples and devotees
of Bhagavan Nityananda

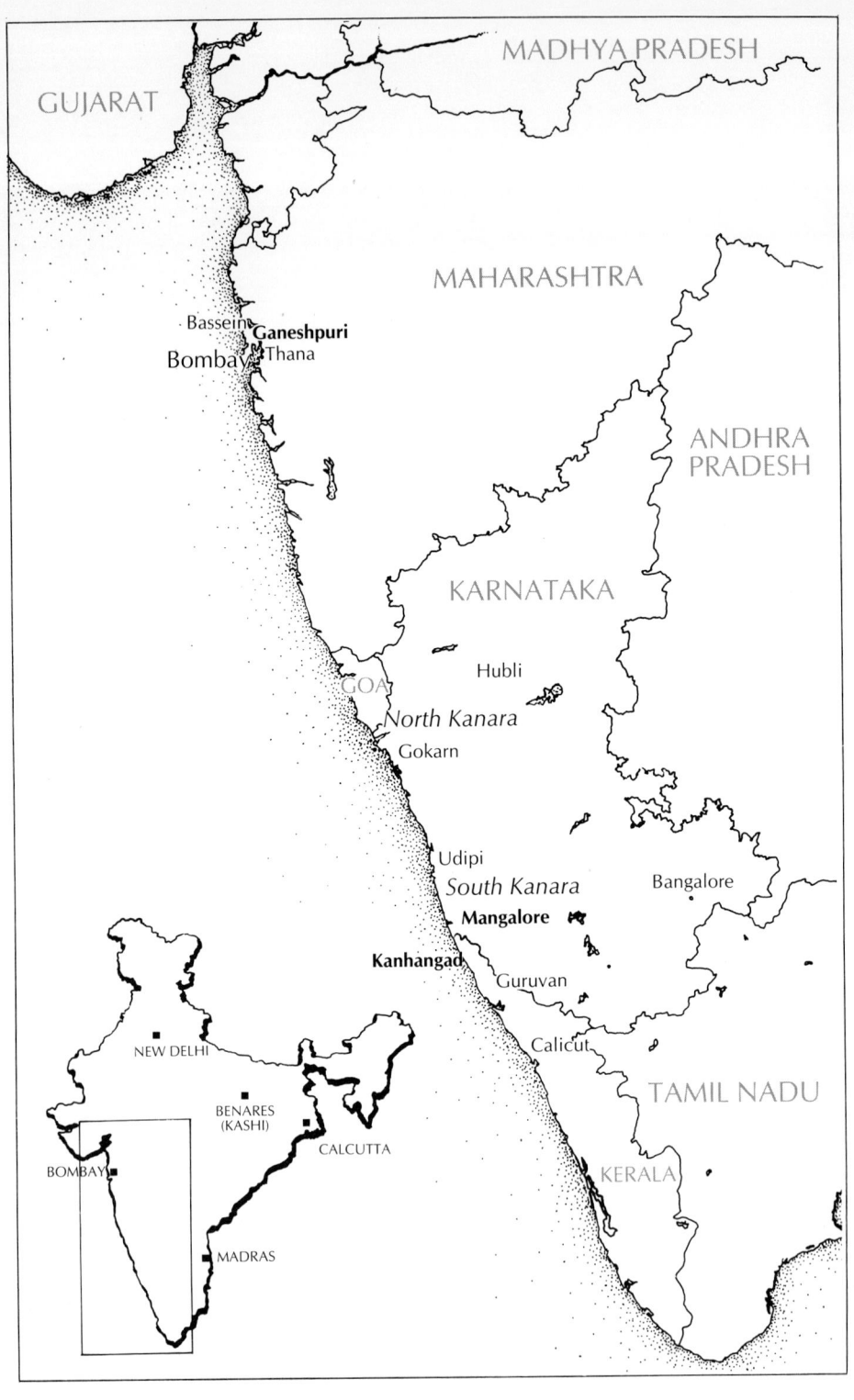

Contents

viii   About M.U. Hatengdi
 ix   Preface by *M.U. Hatengdi*

  2   About Swami Chetanananda
  3   Introduction by *Swami Chetanananda*

Atman
31   The Stories
33   The Sutras

Buddhi
73   The Stories
75   The Sutras

Omkar
101   The Stories
103   The Sutras

Sadhana
119   The Stories
123   The Sutras

183   Commentary

197   Glossary
205   Index

About The Authors

Captain M. U. Hatengdi was born in Mangalore, India, in 1914. His early education was in the local G. H. School and Government College, and he obtained his Honours/Masters degree in Economics from Presidency College, Madras, in 1936. Joining the Indian Navy in 1941, he retired in 1964. At the time of his retirement, Captain Hatengdi was the Naval Secretary at Naval Headquarters, New Delhi. He was immediately appointed Commercial Manager in the government-owned Mazagaon Dock and soon after was selected as the General Manager and Chairman of the Board of Administration of one the largest buying and selling agencies of the government, known as the Canteen Stores Department, from which he retired in July, 1970. He has since been interesting himself in activity connected with social organizations and religious trusts.

Captain Hatengdi had his first darshan of Bhagavan Nityananda in 1943 and has remained a loving devotee throughout the years. He has served as Chairman of the Sri Nityananda Arogyashram Trust, which established and maintains a charitable hospital in Ganeshpuri. Captain Hatengdi is also the author of *Nityananda: The Divine Presence* (Rudra Press, 1984), a book of stories and reminiscences about the life of Nityananda.

Preface

by
M.U. Hatengdi

The rivers in the east flow eastward, the rivers in the west flow westward, and all enter into the sea. From sea to sea they pass, the clouds lifting them to the sky as vapor and sending them down as rain. And as these rivers, when they are united with the sea, do not know whether they are this or that river, likewise all creatures when they come back from Brahman (God Infinite), know not whence they came.
Chandogya Upanishad

In an attempt to project, in English, an image of the immortal Master of Ganeshpuri, I collected a number of authenticated stories covering a period of nearly four decades, illustrative of the life of Nityananda. Thanks to the interest evinced by Swami Chetanananda of the U.S. and the editorial efforts of the Nityananda Institute in Cambridge, Massachusetts, these were presented to the Western reader in *Nityananda: The Divine Presence*, published by Rudra Press in 1984.

Although that book contained words spoken by Nityananda at Ganeshpuri and published for the first time, I was aware of the inherent inadequacy of words in defining a Divine personality. Such a comprehension is generally held to come only to minds imbued with purity of motives and with a keen inclination towards attaining yoga. Hence Nityananda's exhortation to devotees or even first visitors to cultivate *shuddha bhavana* (purity of motive) and *shraddha* (keen inclination towards yoga). As Krishna says in the *Bhagavad Gita*,

> "Fools pass blindly by the place of my dwelling
> Here in the human form, and of my majesty
> They know nothing at all,
> Who am the Lord, their soul."

In Nityananda's case, the situation was further confused by his silence toward the general public, and the resulting anonymity surrounding his physical manifestation, movements, and activities.

Hence this attempt at a fresh English rendering of these words, originally called the *Chidakash Gita*, and attributed to him in his youthful days in Mangalore some time in the period 1922-24. During this period, he would start a monologue in whichever devotee's house he happened to find himself at that particular moment. After some time he would stop. At first, the listening devotees mistook what he said for gibberish, but later, they discovered two special points connected with these monologues. First, the words so uttered contained pearls of wisdom. Considering that Nityananda was illiterate in the academic sense, they inferred that he could have only uttered them from an exalted state of personal experience. Second, these monologues were invariably preceded by a hailing of Arjuna (the hero of the *Mahabharata* and the one to whom the dialogue known as the *Bhagavad Gita* was revealed by Krishna), asking him to come and listen to Krishna. The actual words he used were: "Arjuna-mama, come and listen, Krishna-ajja is going to speak." The suffix "mama" means, literally, maternal uncle; "ajja" means grandfather.

As a result, devotees started keeping paper and pencils handy, to take notes as soon as Arjuna was hailed. As the places where such monologues took place were not always the same, the devotee recorders, who were by no means highly literate, were not the same, either. But all of them were devout, sincere, and had the highest respect for the youthful Nityananda. This must have helped them in recording, as he was not always very coherent, speaking as if from a trance-like condition. After some time, these monologue sessions stopped completely. At this stage, a senior lady devotee known as

Tulsiamma collected and collated the notes taken down by the several devotees; all of them then turned to Nityananda for instructions about their publication. He told them that the words had come from "chidakash" (ether of awareness or a state of cosmic consciousness), and were not spoken in order to be taken down, printed, or published. Whether they were printed or not, read or not, he ("this one" as he would have said, since he never referred to himself in the first person) was disinterested.

However, Tulsiamma got the notes published in Kanarese, as *Chidakash Gita*, (Song from the Sky of Consciousness). Strictly speaking, the words spoken are more appropriately called *srutis* (divinely revealed wisdom), rather than "gita" which means song or poem. Subsequently, quite a few Kanarese translations, and two English ones, appeared, one English version in 1940 and the other in about 1963. I undertook a fresh English rendering of these selected sutras, not only in an attempt to make the deeper meanings underlying these laconic expressions available to the common man, but also to supplement *Nityananda: The Divine Presence* in portraying his image. The stories in that earlier book are like so many floral tributes, providing through their hue and fragrance, a mosaic image as it were, of a great mystic personality. In this publication, his actual sayings bring out a clearer image, as the words are not from books but from his own experience while in a state of cosmic consciousness.

While the Nitya Sutras describe the qualities of an ideal Guru, I would like to add the qualities of an ideal devotee as given by a South Indian saint. Such a devotee is described by him as being born like Faith incarnate, with an intense longing for the ultimate union of the individual with the Universal. Second, he is oblivious of any special talents or attainments he may be possessing: he would always sing the glories of his Master. Third, he is like a flute in the hands of his Master acting reflexly or automatically as guided by him. Next he will be like the hospitable cowherd who would milk the cow and distribute the milk to the needy: here the Guru is the cow, the milk his knowledge and the needy are the hungering devotees. Finally such a devotee is superior to camphor. The analogy has reference to the purity of camphor and its being used for waving a light (*arati*) before deities in temples and shrines. But whereas camphor burns itself out lighting up the deity for a time, the ideal devotee by his tributes to the Master immortalizes him for all time to come.

Nityananda was not an organization man. He was the silent saint, whose thoughts live through eternity, entering deep into human hearts and brains throughout the world, raising up men and women to achieve varying degrees of success in giving them practical expression in the workings of their lives. He was the type to help and inspire the maximum number, be they householders, men of the world, or renunciates, to the maximum extent, without any overt aids and whether one was close to him physically or not. Hence he consoled a grieving devotee, who had an intuitive premonition of the saint's passing away three months before the actual day, that more could be achieved in the subtle than in the gross. Practically all of the hundreds of devotees that now throng to his samadhi shrine daily never saw him in his physical form. And yet when you enquire of them as to why they come, each one has a tale to tell in which some distress was relieved, guidance received, or elevation of spirit experienced.

In this publication also, the editors of the Nityananda Institute have been a great help, by their persevering editorial efforts with genuine love for the manuscript. They have helped in pruning the rather elaborate commentaries I had provided with extraneous references, so that the pregnant words of the original could shine on their own without being clouded by semantics. I am grateful to them and to Swami Chetanananda for getting these books published in the U.S.

If the two companion volumes achieve even to a limited extent the projection of Nityananda's occult image and help one to veer round towards appreciating eternal values, by attempting to live up to them in a fast changing and troubled world, I would have more than achieved my aim in compiling and writing them.

> "Sir," said a pupil to his master, "teach me the nature of Brahman (God infinite)." The master did not reply. When a second and third time he was importuned, he answered: "I teach you indeed, but you do not follow. His name is silence."
>
> from Shankara's commentary on the *Kena Upanishad*

About The Proceeds:
Sri Nityananda Arogyashram Trust

Shortly before Bhagavan Nityananda's mahasamadhi in 1961, some devotees brought him a proposal for a hospital at Ganeshpuri. Nityananda not only approved the proposal, but he immediately called for the plan of the Ashram estate and pointed out where the land was to be donated for the hospital site. He also indicated that the hospital should be built in three stages, illustrating with his hands: "First small, then bigger, and then very big." The Sri Nityananda Arogyashram Trust was constituted in 1963, and the cornerstone for the hospital was laid in 1966. The only hospital within about thirty kilometers, it serves an estimated population of 50,000 people, most of them poor villagers. Staffing for the hospital is currently being donated by Dr. Manek H. Pavri, who is the daughter of one of the original proposers. Funds are urgently needed for the continuing management of the hospital, and it is in response to this need that Captain Hatengdi has pledged the royalties from the sale of this book to the Sri Nityananda Arogyashram Trust.

NITYA SUTRAS

The Revelations of Nityananda
from the Chidakash Gita

About The Authors

Swami Chetanananda is an American meditation master in the lineage of Nityananda and an initiate of the ancient Saraswati order of monks. His deep, transcendent understanding of the wisdom of Nityananda and his comprehensive background in the philosophy of Hinduism (particularly Kashmir Shaivism) are combined with a truly Western perspective. Expressed in a simple, clear, and direct style, Swamiji's introduction and commentaries use terms that make sense to people raised in modern Western culture.

Swami Chetanananda is Abbot of the Rudrananda Ashram and Director of the Nityananda Institute in Cambridge, Massachusetts. The Rudrananda Ashram is a community of people living a practical spiritual life. Its teaching and meditation practice are derived from the ancient Kashmir Shaivite traditions. The Ashram is named for Swami Rudrananda, an American spiritual teacher who was deeply influenced by his contacts with Nityananda and who was initiated into the Saraswati order of monks by Swami Muktananda. Swami Chetanananda assumed leadership of the Ashram on Rudrananda's passing in 1973. The Nityananda Institute is a not-for-profit center for meditation and quality living committed to making a spiritual life both understandable and accessible to Americans. It is named in loving gratitude for Nityananda of Ganeshpuri.

Swami Chetanananda is also the author of *Songs from the Center of the Well* (Rudra Press, 1983), a book of short verses that celebrate Life with love and wisdom.

INTRODUCTION

For centuries the West has seen India as a land of magic and mystery. Western writers describe fiery-eyed mystics performing apparent feats of magic, while in other circles a rigorous scholarship in philosophy has been pursued with energy and precision for thousands of years. It is a land of stunning and overwhelming contrasts. But of all India's extraordinary and mysterious features, one of the most amazing is that every fifty years or so, she is gifted with the presence of a great being, a *mahatma*. A mahatma is born a totally pure being, innately free of any attachment whatsoever to the world and to the things of the world. Because the mahatma is completely immersed in the Divine and universal, the flow of energy through such a person is remarkable. Nityananda was one of these: a great being, a mahatma, a man of incredible, awesome, yogic power and capacity.

This presence that was Nityananda had very little to do with his body. It had everything to do with the great spiritual force of which his body was merely a beacon. His body was simply a sign pointing to the deep and endless well of spiritual power, and that well does not belong to any personality.

Americans do not think easily in these terms. Although the West has seen many gurus in the last several decades, we really have no idea who or what Nityananda was, because Nityananda's state was something completely different from our ordinary experience. Among the gurus who have appeared here, only a few were very great beings. Many were great showmen, and a few were charlatans. As a result, Americans question deeply both the nature of the guru and the need for the guru. We have no preparation whatsoever for someone like Nityananda. There are no precedents in our culture, no criteria by which to classify a person whose very nature is detachment.

Nityananda did not have a purpose in the world, he had no message to bring. Why he appeared is unknown to anyone except perhaps himself. He was born to the austerity in which he lived his life; simplicity and detachment were his nature, not something he trained for or had to think about. His greatness was completely natural to him.

Yet to us, detachment as thorough as Nityananda's is totally unfamiliar, even shocking. For example, people often brought him offerings of fruit. By the end of a week, these offerings could add up to tons of fruit. Often Nityananda just let the fruit rot. It wasn't that he was stingy or didn't want to give it away; in a way, he didn't even notice that it was there. He was that disinterested in the external. All the fruit and all the flowers and other gifts that appeared were like the raindrops that poured down from the sky. It didn't occur to him to do anything with the rain and it didn't occur to him to do anything with the other gifts that manifested around him.

Most of us think that in order to pursue a spiritual life, we need something different from what we already know; a different idea, philosophy, or life style. Nityananda made no such demands. He was not the promoter of a particular life style, philosophy, or perspective. He was not a teacher of any method and he did nothing at all to establish any kind of organization around him. He never gave any programs, intensives, workshops, or seminars, and he never asked for any money. People came to him, and he blessed them, uplifted them, and gave them whatever they were able to take from him. It was just that simple and that free.

He brought tremendous peace and betterment to the simple people, the poor and the destitute, who were especially drawn to his simplicity and lack of judgment. As time went on, he touched the lives of countless people of all classes, bringing miraculous

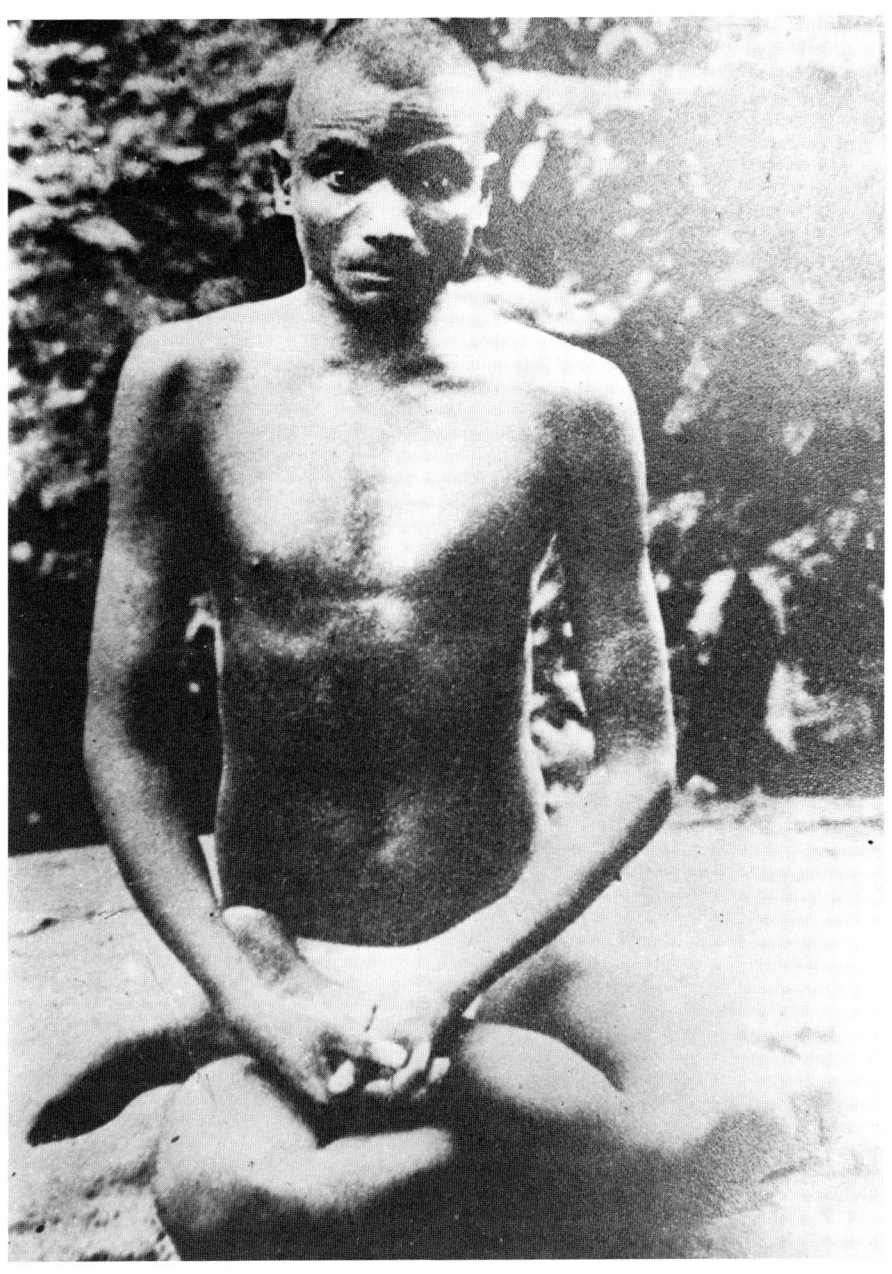

Mangalore, c. 1919: Nityananda told a devotee, "Why waste your breath in gymnastics? Concentrate on this photo and the pranayama will come automatically."

healing and upliftment to many. He never sought any approval, recognition, or promotion for this. He lived in the jungle; people had to seek him out. He was a very simple man who dedicated his life to the presence of the Divine and who, every day, lived as a beacon of that presence.

For us as Americans, it is necessary to suspend judgment as we approach Nityananda's story and words; his words are profound and the subject is nothing less than the essence of life itself.

THE BACKGROUND

Nityananda lived from the late nineteenth century to 1961, and so is one of the most recent of these extraordinary Indian saints. Nonetheless, information about his birth and early childhood is sparse and contradictory. In *Nityananda: The Divine Presence* (Rudra Press, 1984), the following version of his early life is given. The infant Nityananda is found in the jungle of Guruvan by a *harijan* woman who sells the baby to the childless Unniamma of Calicut, a simple woman who earns a small income through household work for Mr. Ishwar Iyer. Mr. Iyer is both a prominent solicitor and a kindly, devout man—he takes an interest in the youngster, named Ram by his adoptive mother, and on the woman's death takes over protection of the child.

Occasional remarks made by Nityananda through the years could support another version as well:

The infant Nityananda, protected by a large serpent that is coiled around him, is found on a river bank. He is taken up by the kindhearted but very poor Unniamma, who in this version is married and has several children of her own. Mr. Iyer again appears as her employer and upon Unniamma's death takes in the orphaned Ram.

A few stories of his boyhood pranks survive; they are also recounted in *Nityananda: The Divine Presence*, which is the companion volume to this book. It is generally agreed that Ram (as he was then known; Nityananda was not applied to him as a name until much later in his life) left his home with Mr. Iyer after the two took a trip to Benares. Nityananda was then perhaps in his early teens. It is known that he traveled widely during this period. Although it is impossible to reconstruct an itinerary, it is thought he spent considerable time in the Himalayas and also in many holy

Bombay, c. 1927: Nityananda with the family of devotee Sitaram Shenoy.

places in Northern India. When Mr. Iyer was dying, Nityananda returned to Calicut, to be with his foster father in his final days. Shortly after the funeral, Nityananda again departed, this time for a period of wandering in Southern India. There are many stories of even more far-ranging travel: to Singapore and Malaysia, even Japan.

Whether or not Nityananda had a guru has been a source of considerable discussion. It is my belief that everybody has a guru. Even though Nityananda didn't talk about it, and even though there is conflict about how it may have come about, in my opinion, there was undoubtedly someone who first breathed into Nityananda this awakening of his own inner spiritual force. This force is like an oilwell: there is great, intense power and pressure in an oilwell all the time, but the force has to be tapped. When it is tapped, all the immense richness explodes to the surface very powerfully. In the same way, someone tapped the well in Nityananda. Whether it was a long association or a momentary meeting, whether it was Ishwar Iyer or someone in the Himalayas or in Singapore, or Shivananda, or this one or that one, I don't know. And it doesn't really matter, it is not important. What is important is that a contact did take place, that the well was tapped and the greatness therein came to the surface, where it continues to have a powerful effect in our lives.

Beginning around 1910, more and more stories place the young Nityananda in the South Kanara district of North Kerala. This was a time of miracles, and growing recognition that an exceptional being was present. Nityananda was officially "discovered" in Udipi in 1918 by two gentlemen who remained life-long devotees.

During this period, Nityananda traveled a great deal, although he also stayed for a time in contemplation at Guruvan, the jungle where it is said he was found as an infant. A few miles further toward the sea is Kanhangad, and here also Nityananda stayed for a time, starting several substantial building projects and doing much work on the rock-cut caves for which the area is famous. An ashram developed around him in Kanhangad, for by this time he was quite well known. There are now temples to his honor at both Guruvan and Kanhangad.

It was during the early 1920s in Mangalore that he spoke the words translated here. Nityananda had many devotees in Mangalore, and it was his custom to stay with a devotee family in the town, while the other local devotees came to sit with him in the evenings. Several photographs from these years are reproduced in this volume, one showing Nityananda sitting with the families of his devotees.

In the mid-thirties, he finally settled in a jungle called Ganeshpuri, near Bombay. He remained at Ganeshpuri for almost thirty years, until his *mahasamadhi* in 1961. His reputation grew steadily during this time. He drew great crowds to this tiny place in the jungle. When Nityananda first arrived in Ganeshpuri, he stayed at a very old Shiva temple, called the Bhimeshwari temple. At that time the temple was overgrown by the surrounding jungle and inhabited by snakes and tigers. Nityananda cleared it out and settled there. The temple was very simple. It was built in the sixth or seventh century, and was just a hollow place lined with stones, with a

Kanhangad: Flag marks present temple location. The steps were cut from the rock by Nityananda himself.

The rock-cut caves at Kanhangad. This center aisle is open at both ends and has many small chambers on either side.

Ganeshpuri, 1982: Ancient Bhimeshwari Temple dedicated to Shiva. The central lingam is topped by a cobra image and adorned with flowers.

Ganeshpuri, 1961: Nityananda's mahasamadhi procession.

roof overhead. In the center was a *lingam*, a rounded post made of stone that is the iconography for Shiva as pure potential. The villagers used to pour water over it and decorate it with flowers and *kumkum*, the vermilion powder used in worship and ceremonies.

Simply because he was there, the sixty or seventy miles around Ganeshpuri became totally transformed from a jungle to a place where cultivated people lived and rich ground was developed. So many things happened because of his greatness.

Nityananda's life remained austere and simple; he was an *avadhut*. Many people considered him to be an incarnation of Ganesha, the son of Shiva and Parvati. He lived as a total renunciate (*sannyasi*). He wore only a loincloth. For years he only took food from someone else's hand, and the food he did eat was very simple: some fruit, a few vegetables, a little coffee—that was all. He spent his days in meditation. In his later life, even while receiving thousands of people for *darshan*, his state remained the same.

Just from his presence, miracles flowed. Nityananda never claimed credit for any miracles that happened around him—miracles of healing, of understanding, of the bestowal of peace and joy—instead, he gave all credit to God and to the faith and devotion of the seeker. "Everything that happens, happens automatically by the will of God," he would say.

For him, everything was possible. Miracles occurred naturally around him because he was always in a state of perfect Self-realization, always in union with the inner Self. This simple truth, the need for this union, was at the heart of his teaching.

In its essence, Nityananda's teaching is profoundly simple. Like the ancient sages of many traditions, he said that anyone who merges the individual into the universal is an enlightened person. The goal of *sadhana* (spiritual practice) is to merge the individual consciousness into the divine consciousness, to merge *Shakti*, creative energy, into *Shiva*, the seat of consciousness.

Thus, a person established in the Supreme, or what Nityananda called the *chidakash*, puts an end to all wandering, and to all the multiplicities that are manifest in the Self. A person who lives in the Self lives beyond space and beyond time. A person who lives there dwells in infinity, where all past lives are known and put to an end, and where all past karmas are dissolved. The life of such a person is the pure, very beautiful, fully abundant experience of the supreme Self.

The Sutras

The Nitya Sutras demonstrate Nityananda's mastery of spirituality; he speaks with simple conviction about the most subtle and refined points of the spiritual realm. And because Nityananda spoke very little, these sutras are a rare treasure of inspired wisdom, spoken from a special state of consciousness.

The Sutras date from the early 1920s in Mangalore, as mentioned above. Devotees would gather around Nityananda each evening. Most of these times were spent in silence, but occasionally Nityananda would speak from a trance-like state. It was some time before the devotees realized that his speeches were filled with great wisdom; they then began to take down his words. It must be remembered that there were many different note-takers, often of different dialects and different levels of education. Some sutras were not put on paper until after Nityananda had stopped speaking for that evening. Years later, these various notes were gathered and compiled by a devotee and published in the Kanarese dialect. Since then, other translations and versions have appeared in several languages and dialects, including two previous English versions.

These sutras are not to be taken as definitive statements to be studied from an intellectual point of view. To do that would be to miss the spirit of this endeavor. We have brought this book to the public to give people some direct contact with Nityananda's wisdom, and to reveal to some extent what was going on in his mind, what he did, and what his spiritual practices were. But to try to define every word and to try to put every word into some context would be a mistake. Nityananda first and foremost was concerned with the immersion of the mind in the inner Self. He had no concern with consistency or intellectual acuity. There is no record of Nityananda receiving any formal education outside of Mr. Iyer's home. He was not an intellectual or a scholar, nor was he exactly a teacher, since he did not try to inspire anyone's mind. He only lived in and from the Self—that was his whole interest.

He was not concerned about the differences that existed among systems and philosophies. His language was not rigorously philosophical; whether a term was Vedantic and from the school of Shankara, whether it was Tantric, or Buddhist, didn't matter to him. Nityananda's vision was universal and he used language common people would understand. Occasionally visitors to Ganeshpuri would try to engage him in scholarly debate, but to no avail: "What is there in the *Gita*? From beginning to end, it is advice to renounce, renounce, and renounce. What else is there?" he told one *Gita* scholar. When Nityananda used the words "Vedanta" or "Veda," he was not referring to Vedanta as a specific philosophical system, but as a synonym for truth and knowledge: Veda as knowledge, and Vedanta as the goal of the Vedas. Thus, Nityananda used terms from all the great traditions of India, without distinction.

THE PHILOSOPHY

"The essential knowledge must be attained by everyone. What is this essential knowledge? For the individual Self to know the mystery of the universal Self." (Sutra 51)

Both the mystery and the wisdom of Nityananda's words arise from the same understanding: everything is one. To fulfill the requirement for liberation, to merge the individual in the Divine, we must understand that there is no inherent difference between the two. The apparent difference, and thus all the confusion and multiplicity of life, is in fact simply a mis-understanding: *maya*. The life-force, the dynamic creative energy that is the source and sustenance of our individual lives, is the same creative energy that moves in all things and in all places. Thus, the study of yoga is the study of the Self, of our own life-force. The more we study it, the more we realize that there is nothing outside of it. The simple, fundamental ground of our own being permeates all that is. All experience manifests on the same field of pure consciousness, and this consciousness that moves in us moves in everyone and everything. The Self *is* the Absolute, and we have intimate, personal access to it.

The Nature of the Absolute

"Shiva-Shakti is the Shakti of the indivisible Parabrahma, and Parabrahma Shakti is the Self. This is the One reality." (Sutra 63)

The Absolute, the Ultimate Reality, the highest of all, is pure consciousness. This pure, dynamic consciousness is the ground and source of all manifestation, large and small. Many names have been given to this "ground of all": Shiva, Parashakti, Parabrahma, Atman, the Self, God. It is the divine consciousness in all, the one consciousness. This ocean of pure potentiality has two inseparable aspects: pure potential (Shiva), and pure energy (Shakti). Shakti is the supreme creative aspect of the Absolute, vital and dynamic. It is both completely stable and never still, eternally pulsating, throbbing, vibrating. Nityananda called this pulsation Omkar: the creative energy of Life. Within the sea of pure consciousness, this resonance causes movement, waves and ripples that intersect and mingle, rise and break. All manifestation arises from the movement and interaction of forces precipitated by the resonance that is Omkar. Omkar is the original word (*Paravac*), the universal sound (*Shabda*), the Word in the Gospel of St. John: "In the beginning was the Word and the Word was with God and the Word was God" (John 6:1). In the *Rig Veda*, one of the most ancient of Indian holy texts, Omkar is *Vac*, creator and substance of all. Omkar is pulsating everywhere and always at the same time. It has no inherent form. It is completely open, pure potential.

> "The OM-sound vibrates like a storm in the sky. It has neither beginning nor end. All that is, is born of OM." (Sutra 95)

Omkar (Shakti) is the very nature of the Absolute, the nature of God. The vibration of Omkar gives rise to the whole universe; it is a living energy. Synonymous with the OM-sound and *pranava*, Omkar is the universal, all pervasive, all permeating Mantra. This one dynamic impulse reverberating within itself gives rise to all experience: intellectual, volitional, emotional, and spiritual.

Omkar is also described as *sat-chit-ananda*: being-consciousness-bliss. The Absolute is that which *is*. Eternally stable, it is self-luminous, conscious force, and it is continuously, joyously manifesting its own awareness: sat-chit-ananda.

> "The universe arises from sound; from sound, form arises, and all things that have form." (Sutra 92)

Exactly how this vibrant, self-aware, ever-pulsating ocean of pure consciousness manifests as our familiar material world is the subject of much scholarly debate. In general, all schema trace a hierarchical development beginning with the single Absolute that manifests in ever more differentiated levels. For Nityananda also, the material world is the most differentiated, the most gross, level. Each successive level is contained within its more subtle predecessor. Thus, all things are ultimately composed of certain basic elements that are the first, most subtle, differentiations from the Absolute.

> "When the life-energy moves in an outward direction, desires are born. There follows the mind, which divides and subdivides into the two-, four-, and six-fold gunas, and what is called 'the world' comes into being." (Sutra 70)

Nityananda spoke primarily of two sets of such elements: the five categories of earth, water, fire, air and ether, and the three primary *gunas* (constituent elements of *Prakriti*, cosmic Nature): *sattva*, *rajas,* and *tamas*. Sattva guna is pure light and perfect balance, while tamas guna is the other end of the spectrum, embodying inertia, darkness, and pure density. Between the two is rajas guna—passion, fire, and dynamic activity.

> "All principles have a single root: Parabrahma, the One Absolute." (Sutra 5)

Omkar is the essence of all of these; it is the "power of doership" of the Absolute, the essence of life, of words and objects, and of human beings. Omkar is the heart of Atman, and Atman is central to the mystery of man's essential nature, because Atman is the Self. In the Sutras, a distinction is made between *jivatman*, the individual Self, and *paramatman*, the divine Self, but the distinction is only on the surface. The distinction is not real, it is maya. This does not mean that the world is an illusion, because the power that underlies everything is real power. Rather, maya implies that nothing is as it appears to be; nothing outside and nothing inside is as it appears to be. The individual is not really separate. Each person is like a wave on the surface of the ocean. Each wave is different, but nonetheless, all are water—only water. An extension of the supreme Self is not in any way different from the supreme Self. Jivatman is the supreme conscious energy expressed as an individuated person, paramatman is the Absolute, and they are both really the same thing. When Nityananda speaks of merging the jivatman into the paramatman, he refers simply to the merging of waves into water: Atman into Atman.

The Nature of the Individual

> *"The difference between the individual and the Universal is like the difference between the river and the sea, it is a difference of degree only."* (Sutra 37)

Within each individual, the structure of the universe is reflected. Whatever the divine consciousness manifests in the universe, the individual consciousness manifests in the form of the human body. Nityananda called the vitality of the Absolute, Omkar or Shakti. As this energy moves out from the source, it becomes distinguished (but not separated) from it. As the essence of the individual jivatman, it is called *kundalini*.

> *"Just so the life-force (Shakti, kundalini) is the same in all creatures, mobile and immobile. The sun and moon also are the same life-force."* (Sutra 11)

Kundalini is the all-encompassing energy of life itself. In the individual, it has three aspects that are one dynamic event manifesting on three levels: biological, subtle or psychic, and purely spiritual. The energy of our biological existence is *prana* kundalini. The energy that supports the intellectual and emotional manifestations of our being is *chitta* kundalini, the mind. The third aspect, *para* kundalini, is the condensed manifestation of pure consciousness; it is the same as Shakti, the same as Omkar. These aspects relate to different stages or states of consciousness; while they manifest in different ways, the essence of each is the same paramatman. Awareness of this essence is liberation.

> *"Awaken the kundalini-shakti through the breath; when it is roused, liberation is possible."* (Sutra 20)

Pranakundalini, or simply prana, is the driving force of our psycho-physical mechanism. It is the breath within the breath, the "breath of life." Not the same as the physical breath, it is more accurate to say that prana is the link between the mental and the physical. Thus, mind (*manas*) plays an important role in the unfoldment and expansion of the inner vision, since mind and breath are intimately related. The thoughts and feelings that arise and subside in the mind do so on the movement of this subtle breath of life. The practice of *pranayama* uses the mind to control prana while simultaneously using prana to control the mind. The aim of this practice is to bring the flow of subtle energy into the awareness and control of the individual.

> *"Of the nadis, three are most important: the ida, pingala, and sushumna. Sushumna is the seat of kundalini."* (Sutra 85)

This flow of energy takes place within a structure that is sometimes called the subtle body, with prana corresponding to the subtle breath. In the Sutras, Nityananda speaks of the three primary nerves or *nadis*: the *ida*, the *pingala*, and the *sushumna*. They are channels in the subtle body for the flow of conscious energy. The nadis are arranged like the familiar medical symbol of the caduceus: a straight central channel (sushumna) is flanked by two side channels (ida and pingala) that criss-cross over the center like a loose braid (see diagram, page 18). At each point of cross-over, there is a center, a *chakra*.

> *"The subtle is in the chakras, in the subtle tube. Within the subtle tube is the kundalini shakti, the kundalini shakti and the subtle tube are OM."* (Sutra 47)

A chakra is a point in time and space where various flows of energy interact with one another and create a resonance that is uniquely different from the resonance of the individual energies that combined to make it. In the human being, these chakras are centers of vibration from which our mental, emotional, and physical characteristics are determined and expressed.

> *"[T]here are seven chakras from the muladhara chakra at the base of the spine."* (Sutra 18)

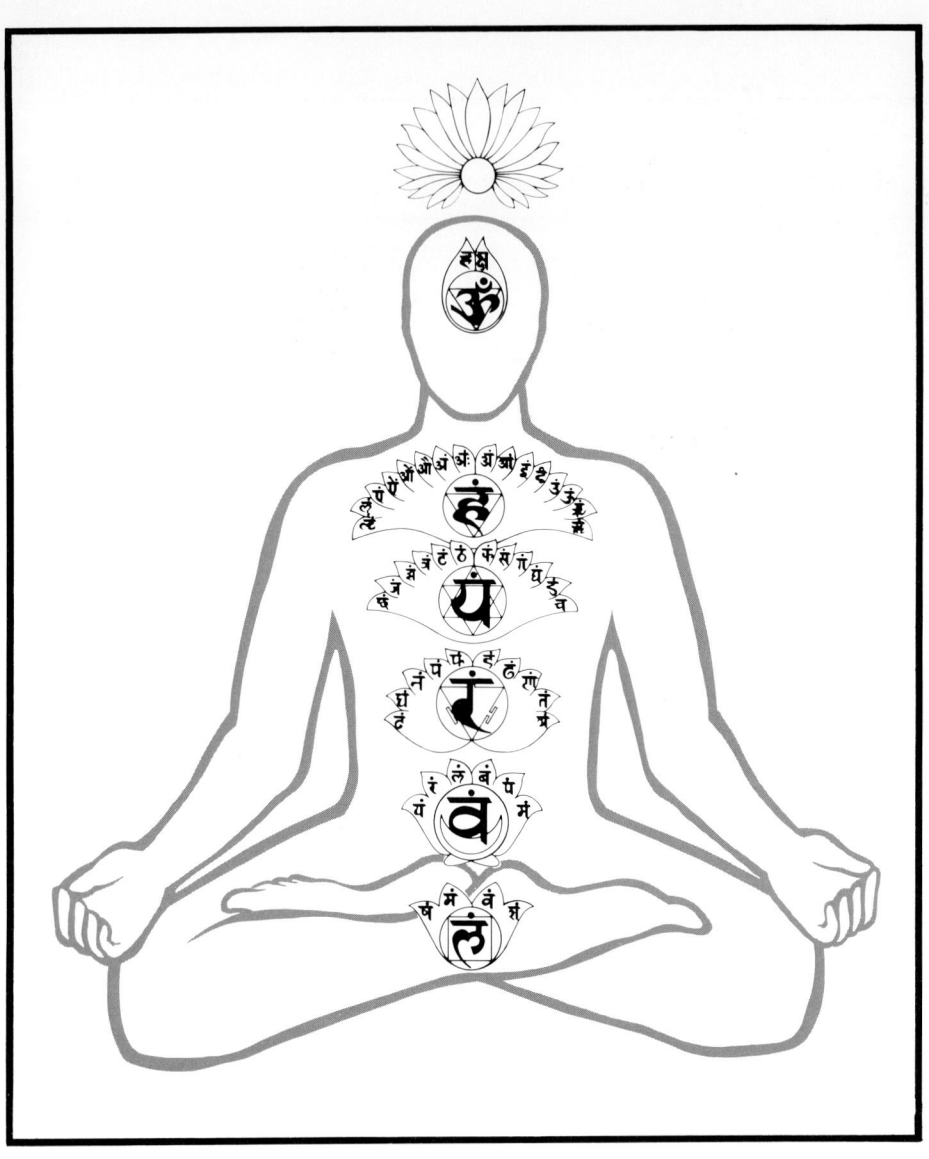

The seven major chakras with their associated mystic symbols and Sanskrit letters.

There are seven major chakras, each one of which corresponds to an area in the physical body: the base of the spine, the base of the sex organs, the navel, the heart, the throat, a point between the eyebrows, and the top of the head. The kundalini energy is said to lie dormant in the *muladhara*, the chakra at the base of the spine; the nadis also originate in the muladhara. In addition to the muladhara, Nityananda specifically refers to the *ajna chakra*, located between the eyebrows, and the *sahasrara chakra*, at the top of the head. The goal of yogic practice is to rouse the sleeping kundalini, allowing it to rise through the nadis and chakras, finally to merge with the Absolute in the sahasrara chakra.

> *"The seat of discrimination is in the sky of the heart. When the kundalini is raised to the heart-space in the head, then the breath is single, the universe is in one's Self. All is in the Atman."* (Sutra 42)

The sahasrara chakra at the top of the head is the seat of Self-realization. It is the junction point between the individual and the Divine, that point in a human being where lies the *dynamic stillness* that is the union of Shiva and Shakti. It is the only part of the psycho-biological mechanism that is still, just as the hub of a wheel is still while the spokes and the rim move around it. It is the place from which all of the spiritual forces that make up a human being are extended, the place the breath comes from, the place the chakras come from, the place the physical body comes from.

> *"The Self is there before you and after you; even before you were born, there was creation. It is you who are not aware."* (Sutra 6)

A human being, then, is really an extension of a spiritual force. The dormant kundalini represents the furthest extension of that energy. As long as it is crystallized in this extension, the person is a limited being and sees things in terms of distinctions. When, through *shaktipat*, the kundalini begins to rise, this crystallization is loosened up. As the energy begins to flow again, it is reabsorbed into itself as the Divine.

"When the individual spirit leads the inner Shiva-Shakti upward to the Brahmarandhra, the individual becomes one with the Indivisible. This is liberation." (Sutra 16)

"Creation is nothing but energy being released or projected from God. Entering back into it is dissolution. Identification with the body is the cause of creation as one sees it. The real dissolution takes place when the individual Self merges and dissolves in the Universal." (Sutra 25)

For Nityananda, the sahasrara chakra is synonymous with the Brahmarandhra, the point of dynamic stillness that equals the union of Shiva and Shakti. When the individual creative energy, in the form of the kundalini, is re-awakened and merged into that point through the various yogic practices, the individual consciousness dissolves into the universal consciousness, and what manifests is a complete state known as the divine inner Self. This is the state of universal consciousness and awareness of the Self as the source of the whole universe.

Chidakasha and hridayakasha refer to the awareness that arises in the state of divine consciousness. In that state we experience the inner as vast, maybe more vast than the whole external universe. Hridayakasha means "heart-space," and the heart referred to is the essence or the heart of the whole universe. Chidakasha is consciousness-space, or the sky of consciousness. The heart-space in the head, the sky of the heart, the Brahmarandhra, all these refer to the same experience of infinite expansiveness.

"The source of liberation is Shiva, the linga in the head is Shiva. It is all OM." (Sutra 13)

This Brahmarandhra is also known in Nityananda's sutras as the linga in the head, the symbol of Shiva. In Indian temples, the linga is a stone or metal object that is said to have a masculine quality, to be completely passive, and to contain the whole universe within itself. The linga arose as a symbol of Shiva because the linga in the head is the abode of Shiva, the source of all that is.

The Process of Liberation

Within a human being there is a vast reservoir of spiritual knowledge and pure capability, yet this great treasure is rarely tapped. Our involvement in the world and our entanglement in the struggle for survival limit our awareness to desires and their objects. Like a kaleidoscope, these desires are continuously changing form; the subtle images of shape and color never allow us to really grasp what we think we are seeing. Unless we recognize the kaleidoscope for the illusion it is, much unhappiness and frustration can result.

> *"Return to the Self within, know your own secret, the universe is inside you, you are inside the universe. The inner Self is the One who dances in all."* (Sutra 65)

This primary paradox of unity and diversity recurs at every level. While the process of liberation appears hierarchical at first glance, the orderly image of a ladder of ever-higher levels breaks down on closer scrutiny. The process is really more like drawing a series of ever-expanding concentric circles, with the *jiva* in the center and the Absolute not only the outermost circle, but also the paper on which it lies and the pen with which it is drawn. This is a deep paradox that cannot be neatly resolved through language. It is only by continuous and deep contemplation that the nature of this paradox can be penetrated and encompassed. What follows is called liberation.

> *"What is called akasha is in the head, the heart-space, the sky of the heart. The Life-Power is One."* (Sutra 37)

Nityananda addressed this paradox indirectly through the image of the heart-space in the head, the chidakash, the sky of the heart. This verbal image brings together what is "above" and what is "below" with an intuitive clarity; in the sky of consciousness, there is no duality and no paradox. The question then is how to reach this center. Nityananda directs the seeker to "the royal road."

> *"A true guru can turn you from the jungle road of ignorance to the royal road of spiritual knowledge."* (Sutra 102)

> "Without the Guru, you cannot reach the goal." (Sutra 9)

The paradox is repeated in the form of the guru, because the guru has two aspects. Nityananda called these the primary/action guru and the secondary/causal guru. On the one hand, there is the physical teacher, a personality to be dealt with and talked to, a person who performs actions that have an effect in the world, a person viewed by some with admiration and by others with disgust. In other words, a human being viewed by ordinary people as the same or less than they are. On the other hand, for those few people who are able to, or care to, look deeply into the situation, what is really there is not a personality at all, but an extraordinary field of spiritual energy. From this field, a human being can draw deep nourishment for his innermost being, and with this nourishment, he can grow into a complete maturity in the supreme state of pure consciousness.

> "The secondary guru leads you to the well. The primary guru drinks from it." (Sutra 104)

The physical aspect of the guru, the secondary teacher, serves us like a doorway. With our diligence, love, and devotion we pass through this doorway of the physical teacher into the level of consciousness that Nityananda calls the action guru. The action guru is the same as Parabrahma, Paramashiva, or chidakasha. At this level, we express the infinite spaciousness, extraordinary power, and creative intelligence that are the characteristics of the essential state of unity from which all experience takes its form.

> "Liberation does not come to search for you, you must seek liberation, you must make the effort." (Sutra 117)

The effort required if you are a sincere seeker of God is to see through the form, to pass beyond the personality and the individuality and the eccentricity of the teacher, and in so doing to transcend your own personality and limitations.

> "Draw the breath up to the Brahmarandhra, kindle the fire, purify the nadis, burn up the impurities. This is the yoga-fire,...the pure energy of the Supreme." (Sutra 28)

The Power within the presence of the guru energizes all levels of a human being. The transmission of this power is called shaktipat, which means "transmission or descent of grace." Shaktipat brings about a quantum leap in awareness that puts us in contact with the innate freedom and spontaneous creative power that is eternally and everywhere present as the source of all. It awakens the deepest potentiality within us, and the kundalini shakti begins its extraordinary unfoldment. As this unfoldment continues, the entire structure of the human being is refined and purified. When iron is subjected to fire, it is freed of its gross crystallization and impurities and reorganizes as the finer, stronger metal of steel. The human being also, through contact with the forge of the guru, becomes purified by the inner fire of kundalini and is established in the supreme state of awareness. Seeing past the form of the physical teacher brings awareness of the power that is functioning as and through the teacher. Stilling the mind in the flow of that power is liberation.

"First silence the mind and establish it in the Self, then concentrate deeply, with spiritual discernment." (Sutra 179)

When the various waves of creative energy that form the mind are stilled and become like the surface of a calm lake, our awareness can penetrate our own depth and recognize the complete oneness of our individual Self and the Divine. Deep contact or connection with a guru enables us to feel so deeply secure and calm that we can begin to turn within and observe the workings of our inner universe without the doubts, fears, and tensions that continuously draw the mind of the ordinary person back into the realm of dualistic awareness.

"Mind is the root of bondage and liberation, of good and evil, of sin and holiness." (Sutra 71)

The mind is both the entity to be stilled and the means of stilling it, for the nature of mind is complex. Nityananda used many different terms to distinguish the facets of the mind. The major distinction is between "manas" and "buddhi," with manas being the ordinary, limited mind, and buddhi the higher mind, the mind capable of subtle discrimination and spiritual discernment. In some of the classical Indian systems, the word *chitta* denotes the whole mental apparatus, composed of three parts: manas, perceiving mind; buddhi, discriminative mind; and ego, the "I-consciousness." Nityananda used "body-idea" and "body-consciousness" synonymously with "I-consciousness." Simple thoughts, feelings, and desires arise in the mind, but the mind is also capable of realizing *jnana* (wisdom), and truth. Jnana is the highest wisdom, the wisdom of the *jnani*, one who has realized the Self. Here again is a paradox, for the wisest person has transcended the mind and its desires: "A jnani has no mind." (Sutra 49)

> *"If your mind is not pure, how can you develop equal-sightedness? If you do not practice, how can you develop balance? Through practice, the subtle intelligence develops and the desire for objects disappears."* (Sutra 141)

As our understanding expands and we begin to see beyond the "body-idea" and beyond the limits of ordinary mind, a sense of detachment also grows. Detachment, desirelessness, and what Nityananda called *vairagya*, perfect dispassion for worldliness, are necessary requirements for the seeker. The Sanskrit word *sannyasi* literally means "he who has cast away" or "a renunciate." However, the meaning of renunciation is also subtle. It is not objects that must be renounced, but the desire for objects; not actions, but attachment to the results of those actions. True renunciation is not of things but of the desire for things. Vairagya is the attitude that leads to a state of understanding in which the true nature of objects is known. Consequently, these objects no longer have any power over a person whatsoever.

> *"When the mind runs after desires, striving is necessary to bring the mind to one-pointedness. Concentrate the mind in buddhi."* (Sutra 80)

Meditation is an integral part of sadhana. Nityananda spoke of meditation as a focused concentration, the merging of mind into wisdom, the look within. The goal is bringing the mind to perfect one-pointedness; achieving this goal tests all the faculties of the seeker. The mind must be stilled and drawn away from desire, the breath must be harmonious and ultimately must become single, and the awareness must reach inside to come in touch with and to observe the action of the kundalini shakti.

> "Like milk being boiled, the prana in the sushumna is heated by intense faith and discrimination and led toward the sahasrara chakra (the still point) in the head. As the kundalini shakti crosses each chakra, each guna changes." (Sutra 21)

Then, as a natural result of the awakening of the inner transforming power, the kundalini shakti rises through the chakras to join and merge into the heart-space, the Brahmarandhra. The love and happiness that then arise within us dissolve all the various tensions and superficial desires, and satisfy our deepest needs. With a full heart, the mind can become still and one-pointed on the power of the divine presence. This is the merging of the individual into the universal and transcendent that Nityananda consistently called the most important purpose of our presence on this earth. To merge heart to heart and spirit to spirit with the guru, in the field of supreme Shiva-Shakti, frees a human being from all mechanistic thinking, and from the bonds of cause and effect. This is the union of the individual and the Divine.

> "Fulfillment is possible only when you merge in this pure heart; there all idea of "you" and "I" disappears. In the chidakash is liberation, shakti, love and devotion." (Sutra 40)

Liberation is the clear, luminous recognition that our mind, emotions, and physical body are nothing more than extensions of the supreme Mantra of God that pulsates silently everywhere and always at once. Everywhere we look, inside and outside, we experience nothing but the extraordinary clarity, beauty, and power of the supreme Self. It is eternally pulsating, creating, absorbing, and manifesting yet again—ourselves, the world, all that is—simply as the fundamental expression of its absolute freedom to do whatever it wants to do; an expression of its supreme freedom and its incredible joy. Sat-chit-ananda.

Conclusion

In all places and in all ages, there are many good people who seek spirituality, who have spiritual understanding, and who have some positive concerns for humanity. Yet in any age there are only a few people, rare and great beings indeed, who can communicate the highest, transcendent state of consciousness to other human beings, and who dwell in that state while still functioning in the world as ordinary (though perhaps eccentric) human beings.

Nityananda was such a rare, gifted being. His spiritual presence flows through his words, for he spoke from a state of complete Self-awareness. By becoming aware of the ongoing pulsation, by remaining aware of it every day, the mind itself becomes a mantra. Whatever is spoken in that state is sacred, pure, and uplifting. In that state, the sounds that come, and the way that the sounds are articulated and joined to form images, is something mysterious and magical, a manifestation of the freedom of our innate, pure consciousness. Nityananda's words came from that state. They inspire us to open our minds and hearts to the extraordinary creative energy which permeates our lives, and to experience, recognize, and appreciate the miracles that happen to us.

Nityananda always said, "When the disciple calls with love, I am there." For people who are willing to open their eyes and hearts, Nityananda is a symbol of the enduring, ever-present power of the Divine in the world. This dynamic spiritual presence has the power to transform lives, to relieve suffering, to grant freedom from poverty and disease, and most importantly, from hard-heartedness. When you are filled with this power, then even in the most simple circumstances, life is an experience of complete fulfillment and happiness. Our lives become an act of service expressed in a state of detachment. When we begin to direct our lives toward the recognition of that supreme creative power that is our essence, then we speak, think, and act from that power. Our lives are in perfect harmony, perfect balance, perfect union with the power of life itself.

Nityananda felt such a life of perfect union was possible for everyone. This is perhaps what impressed me most deeply in these sutras, the simple and total availability of that supreme state to anyone who seeks sincerely. The goal of Nityananda's teaching, and the single most important thing each person can do with his life, is to recognize the creative power within, and dissolve the mind into it. It is clear from these sutras that for Nityananda, this supreme, highest state is not the privilege of special birth nor the exclusive property of some special class of beings. It is available to everyone. The simple purity, the joy, and the extraordinary communion with the Divine that are the outstanding characteristics of Nityananda's life and presence are accessible to everyone: to me and to you.

Thousands of people, sometimes tens of thousands in a day, had the opportunity to experience and participate in the divine presence that was Nityananda. Yet how many people took away something great and enduring from it? Not nearly as many as were there. But Nityananda made it accessible to everyone, there were no barriers. Thus, it is up to us. Through our devotion, love, and diligence, we can grow in our understanding of that simple and perfectly full state that is the field of our individual life and the field of all experience.

The greatest treasure in the whole world is hidden inside each of us. We may or may not be successful in the world, but this treasure we can definitely find. To seek that treasure is a good thing. To find it is the best.

It is really up to you.

Swami Chetanananda

PART ONE
ATMAN

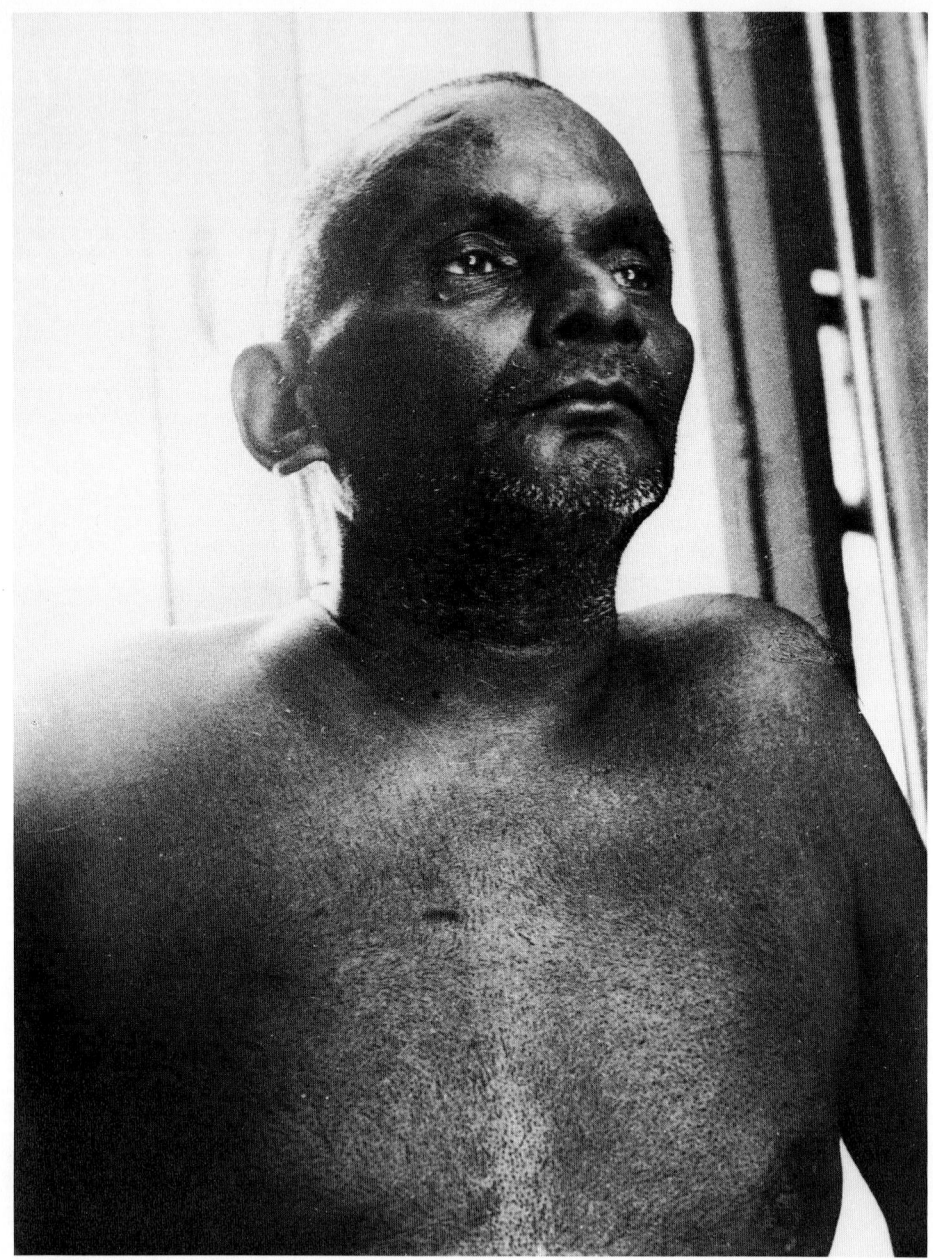

ATMAN

Nityananda always urged his devotees to look inward for the truth. He spoke of the royal road to liberation as being within and often said that the best place for pilgrimage is in the heart. Even in such matters as demonstrations of respect, Nityananda stressed the internal, saying that devotion offered from the *sthana* (literally "the place," implying from the heart) always reached him. Once a woman devotee, wishing to show her respect to Nityananda, was rolling on the floor from the entrance of the Ashram to the place where he was sitting. As she started, he said, "This is not necessary. Is it chapati dough? Why roll like that? What is to be rolled up is not the body but the mind and the senses."

In 1929 two young women from Mangalore went to Kanhangad in search of Nityananda. There was only one train in the morning and one in the evening between Kanhangad and Mangalore. The young women searched for the Master all day but could not find him, even though they went most of the way to what is now known as Guruvan. They were making their disappointed return when they suddenly saw Nityananda perched on a tree. They told him they did not know anything about spiritual matters but had come for guidance. "It is the spark, the spark," he repeated from the tree. "Blow it up until it is a blazing fire." Then he added, "Go now or you will miss the train." This simple message sufficed to guide the women, who were devotees from that time forward.

Once Nityananda was asked by a member of the local legislature to define *guru-kripa*, the grace of the guru. He responded with several questions: Where is your home town? How long does it take to get there by road? By sea? By rail? After getting estimates of all these times, Nityananda then asked the legislator how long the trip would take by air, if an airstrip were available. The devotee said it would take less than half an hour. "This is guru-kripa," Nityananda replied, "providing the shortest route and fastest way 'home' to the place of our origin within the Infinite."

THE SUTRAS

The real sunrise is in the sky of the heart, the *chidakash*; 1
this is the most excellent sunrise.
Just as the entire sun is reflected in the water jar,
so the entire universe shines
in the heart-space of the *Atman*.
When you are in a train, the whole world appears to be moving.
Similarly, the whole universe can be known within the Self.*

---

* An asterisk indicates further information can be found in the *Commentary* section.

2   The universal Self is in the individual Self.
Real liberation is to know the subtle in the gross,
the unity in diversity,
the similarity in differences,
the truth in untruth,
the light in darkness,
the life in death.
This is real liberation.

3   You must know your Self.
A true *sannyasi*, a true yogi, has conquered the mind;
he has no mind.
If you enter a dark room after looking at the bright sun,
what do you see?
Nothing.
Look at the Self with the inner eye; you will see the Self
everywhere.

When you get hungry,
you know it yourself.
Everything is known to the Self.

4

All principles have a single root:
Parabrahma, the One Absolute.
To know this principle is *jivanmukti*:
liberation in this life.
You must see the river at its source
not after it merges with the sea.
You must see the central root of the tree
for all trees have only one central root.
All have only one God.
To see all with equal vision is jivanmukti.

5

6

Why do you hold an umbrella?
To protect you from the rain.
Maya (illusion of duality) is the rain and
truth is the umbrella.
A steadfast mind is the handle.
Truth is in everything, but very few have realized it.
Maya comes from Atman, not Atman from maya.
The prime minister is under the king, but he is not the king.
The mind is not the Self, it is the reflection of the Self.
Mind is two grades below Atman.
The mind has an end, Atman has no end.
The mind is often deluded; Atman is not deluded
and is not subject to the *gunas*
(the three primary constituents of all manifestation).
All gunas apply to the mind.
The mind is related to the Atman
as the river is related to the sea.
The Atman is the sea; its water is measureless.
The Atman is without beginning or end.
The Atman does not come and it does not go.
Wherever you turn, it is there.
Nothing else is seen.
The Self is there before you and after you;
even before you were born, there was creation.
It is you who are not aware.*

To search elsewhere for that which you already
hold in your hand is fruitless.
If you light a lamp on the upper floor of the house
and then close all the doors,
no light will be visible below.
"Look at the cinema!" "See the drama!"
But really it is all seen in the head.
Everything can be seen from one place;
It is not necessary to go to different places
to see different things.
The city of Madras can be seen from here
as well as from there.
It is better to see it from one place;
see the form in the head.
The "heart" is not below the neck, it is above.
As we cook, the flames of the fire rise,
so is the heart above.
The heart is full of light, there is no darkness in it.
If a person is beheaded,
it is not easy to identify just the torso.
Only by looking at the face can one be readily recognized.
It is the heart which sees through the eyes;
you must have the inner sight.
What is called the heart-space,
the *hridayakasha*,
the sky of the heart,
is nothing else than the face, which is triangular in form.
You recognize a person by looking at his face.
Know your own secret.
Know your Self.

8   Just as we can see a reflection of the sky
by looking at the still water in a vessel,
so the sky of consciousness can be seen
through the inner eye.

9   If God is in you and you are in God,
maya—creation and dissolution—dissolves in the Self.
There is no maya for those who are free of
the bondage of the three gunas.
He who knows he is not the body is nothing but bliss,
eternal bliss.
The Atman is free of the ideas of honor or dishonor;
the person who gives up these ideas has reached the goal,
he has attained Peace.
In the infinite there is no finite.
Without the Guru, you cannot reach the goal.

For the person firmly established in the One,   10
there is no rebirth.
For such a person, death comes only as he wills.
He has no desires.
To see the One is subtle,
to see the One is to see the same Self in all;
it is "same-sightedness"—the equal vision.
Equal vision sees the One in all by looking inward.
Equal vision sees that this world and the next world are One,
it is the union of *jivatman* and *paramatman*,
the individual and the Absolute.
The jivatman is the modification of the mind,
the paramatman is the great silence:
beyond qualities,
neither good nor evil,
hot nor cold,
formless, qualityless,
No-Thing.

11 If you have come to buy milk, why ask the price of the cow?
If you seek the Self, why be concerned about the body?
One who has attained the Self is in the body
but is not attached to it,
like the dry kernel in the coconut.
When the rope is burnt to ashes, it cannot be used for tying.
No man can harm another.
Each does it to himself with his own thinking.
A boatman is needed to push the barge across the river,
a guru is needed for initiation.
Once the opposite bank is reached,
the boatman's help is not needed.
How is the boat in the water?
So is the Atman in the body.
If your feet are muddy, you will look for water to wash it off.
But if you are afraid to touch the water,
the mud cannot be removed.
One hand alone makes no sound;
when both hands come together, there is sound-energy.
Your fingers are not all the same size, yet when scooping,
they become one.
When there is experience, it is One.
All holy men and perfect ones are alike.
All water in the well is the same,
there are not two kinds of water in the same well.
Just so the life-force (shakti, kundalini)
is the same in all creatures,
mobile and immobile.
The sun and moon also
are the same life-force.

The Atman in chidakash and chidakash in the Atman
are One.
Those who know this One sing in ecstasy.
They know the bliss-producing kundalini.
They discover the kundalini-shakti,
awaken it
and join with it.
By joining with it repeatedly,
devotion and liberation are attained.
Conquer birth and death and forget all,
conquer death and its brood.
Know the true nature of maya,
know also the nature of eternal bliss.
O mind, become one with eternal bliss!
Drink of the Atman in the head,
unite the world with the Atman in the head.
In the head is fulfillment of birth.
Strive for the Atman in the head.
The three states of wakefulness, dream, and sleep
must unite in the Atman.
Keep the key of *buddhi* (discriminative intelligence)
close at hand;
as you guard the key to a treasure,
so with care keep the buddhi in the head.
Water is hot only if it is left on the fire,
on the ground it begins to cool.
Buddhi must be like water on the fire.
Faith must be constant.
Jiva (the Self embodied) is like a calf confined;
as the calf is always eager to escape confinement,
so the jiva is eager to escape into wisdom.

12 Unite meditation, mind, and faith through the subtle *bindu*,
(potentiality at its point of greatest contraction).
Merge in the center of the eyebrows,
and attain oneness.
Following the path of discrimination,
let the pure mind be firmly fixed in *OM* (the univeral sound).
Steady the mind by the practice of pure concentration and
samadhi (state of total absorption in the Self);
become one-pointed.
There is no other means than samadhi
to establish the consciousness in *akasha*, the heart sky.
O jiva, enter the heart sky!
To such a one, the world has no separate existence.
O mind, be free of this body-idea!
To hold the consciousness firm is very difficult
without spiritual practice.
To those who are established in samadhi,
the body is quite foreign. To them,
the gross and the subtle are like the fruit and the seed.
To those established in "I am not the body,"
samadhi is not a separate thing.
For them it is all samadhi, always samadhi, absolute samadhi,
samadhi in *Shiva* (the Absolute), mind-surpassing samadhi.
To one who is submerged in the sweetness of universal wisdom,
the sweetness is not something separate.
The external world has no importance.

The source of liberation is Shiva. 13
The *linga* in the head is Shiva.
It is all OM.
Enlightenment is the most important thing.
Without *nadis* (channels for the flow of subtle breath)
there is no sound.
Love and devotion are the oil, nadi is the wick,
discrimination is the lantern.
Flame, light, and glass are the nadis.
The air-hole is the *Brahmarandhra* (the still point in the head).
The form of discrimination is intelligence.*

Yes, Shiva is in *Kashi*, but Kashi is the sky in the heart. 14
The mind is Kashi,
everything is Kashi,
the eternal Atman is Kashi,
Kashi is in the head.
The ten sounds are eternal; the subtle Kashi is *nirvikalpa*,
the silence of the mind.
Haridwar is the nine gates in the body,
it is in the heart-space.
The heart is the seat of peace.
Yajna (ritual sacrifice) is the tasting of
the nectar of wisdom (*jnanamrita*).*

15   *Yukti* (cleverness or effort) is like traveling on foot.
Shakti is the power that enters the heart;
the spiritual life is like traveling by train.
He who travels on foot will wander,
for the mind (*manas*) is fickle.
The body is the train, the mind is the passenger.
Without passengers, the train will not move,
tickets are not issued,
people do not gather.
There is no first class, nor second, nor third.
Mind is the peace class, buddhi is the driver,
the head is the engine, the nerves and nadis are the gears.
What moves in the nadis is *vayu*, the vital air.*

16   When the individual spirit leads the inner *Shiva-Shakti*
upward to the Brahmarandhra,
the individual becomes one with the Indivisible.
This is liberation, indivisible liberation,
the bliss of the Absolute.
Praise Shiva! In the beginning was Shiva,
in the beginning was Shiva-Shakti alone.
The great protector is eternal bliss,
the great desirelessness is eternal bliss.
You who are without desire,
without the three qualities (gunas),
endowed with virtue, master of your Self, king of jivanmukti,
look within yourself.
The highest form is the human form.
Man is the highest of creatures.
There is nothing higher.
It is man who has created all the countries.*

There are three important nadis17
in the subtle body.
The sun nadi is the *sushumna*,
the moon nadi is the *ida*, the star nadi is the *pingala*.
The sun nadi is red, the moon nadi blue, and
the star nadi green in color.
The ida is on the left, the pingala on the right,
and the sushumna in the center.
The three join at the heart-space.
In time, the OM sound is heard in the head.
This sound, though truly one and undivided,
can manifest as many different sounds:
the roar of the sea,
notes of the flute, violin, or harmonium,
drums, bells, or the buzzing of bees—
the ten sounds.
Yet it is the one subtle sound,
indivisible.*

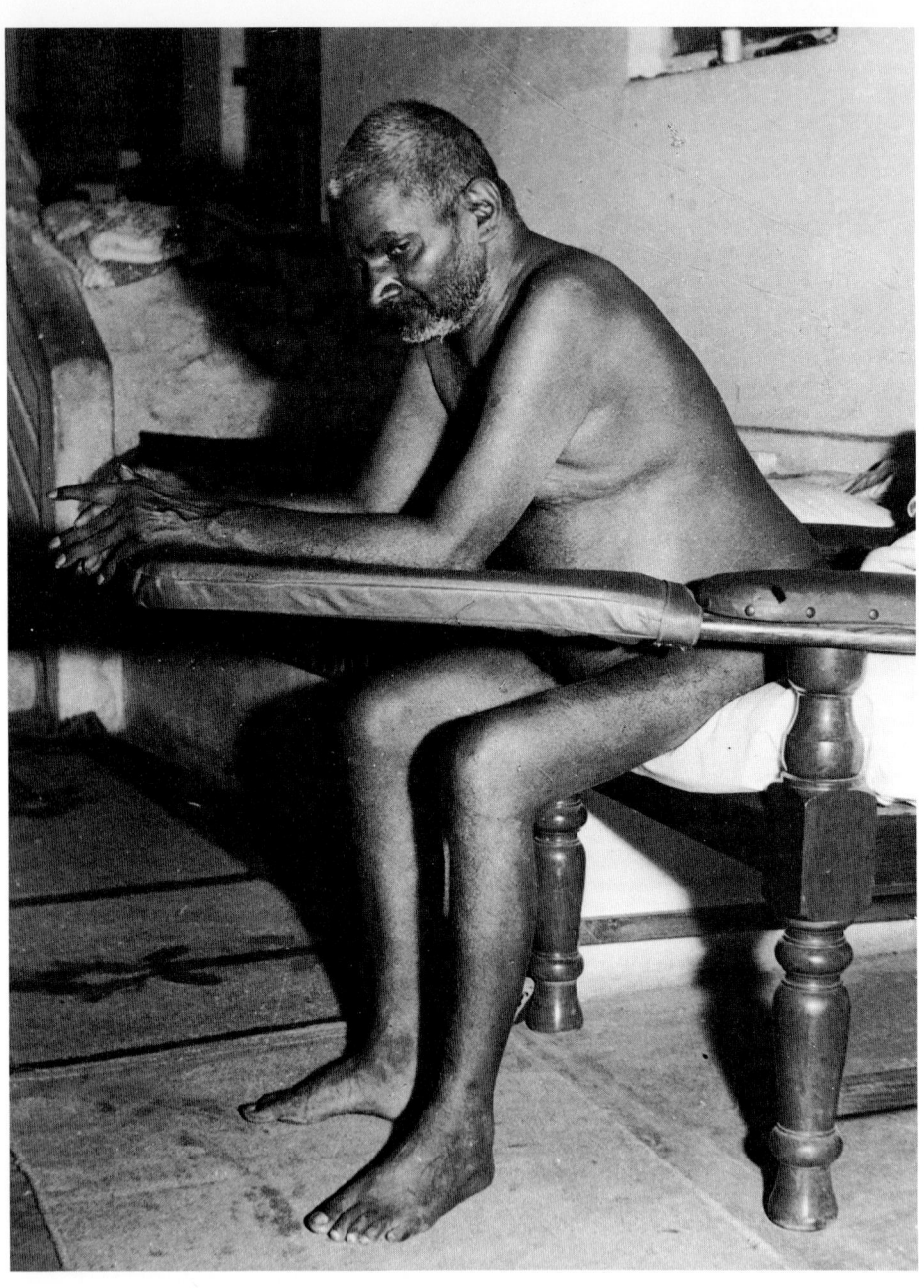

When receiving visitors for darshan, Nityananda would sit with his legs supported on the special extensions of this chair.

The *chakras* below the neck relate to *hatha yoga*.   18
Control over them is acquired through
the intense practice of *pranayama*.
The chakras above the neck relate to *raja yoga*.
Control over them is acquired through
the practice of meditation.
Just as there are seven *chakras* from the *muladhara* chakra
at the base of the spine,
so in raja yoga there are seven chakras above the neck.
In raja yoga the base center is in the throat,
the kundalini has to rise from the throat chakra.
Just as fruit on the coconut tree grows at the top of the tree,
so also the fruit of divine wisdom is experienced in the brain
at the top of the spinal cord.*

The head is the mango.   19
In it is the sweet ambrosia,
the essence of the five senses.
This ambrosia is the supreme energy in man.

20   Awaken the kundalini shakti through the breath;
when it is roused, liberation is possible.
Faith holds the rope of vayu (vital air);
you must hold the rope of vayu tightly.
Bind faith with the rope of *dharana*, perfect one-pointed
concentration.
What is dharana but faith?
Keep the attention constantly on dharana.
Join steadfast faith to perfect concentration and
faith will fill every nerve of the body.
To such a person, there is no separate thing called maya,
the mind itself is maya.
The mind creates all forms:
all matter, all relations, all cause and effect,
light and the universe, all arise from the mind, from maya.
The moment this is realized, all fear of maya disappears.
In meditation, remember your real form.
Stabilize the mind in the practice of meditation,
concentrate the consciousness in the heart-sky;
this is liberation.
The path to liberation is not far from the Self.
Sin and merit are as close as the eye to the ear.
It is not beyond the buddhi,
pleasure and pain are one in buddhi,
the Way of Buddhi leads to liberation.
To steady the mind in one's Self, to be one-minded,
this is liberation.
All wisdom is in the Self.
In the beginning, wisdom is something to be known,
later, wisdom also dissolves in the Self.
Then there is nothing to be said, nothing to be heard,
it is the state of *shunya*, Nothingness.
The subtle breath is like a rope: whether moving in or out,
the movement is the same, it is indivisible,
it is unaffected by time.

Only when entangled with the physical nature
is there difference.
A man gets engrossed in the different properties of the world
and forgets his true nature.
With the help of the subtle intelligence
he can take an upward course.
Steadied by the rope of faith,
the *prana* (subtle breath) turns upward toward liberation,
toward freedom from sense-objects.
Then comes peace.
Reach for that peace, live in this world and the next world.
This is *sat-chit-ananda*, being-consciousness-bliss.
Such a person is eternally free,
free of attachment to the results of work,
free of bondage,
eternally one-minded.
Until the ego-sense of separateness is dissolved,
liberation is indeed far off.
Without the sense of One, there is no yoga, no freedom.
Only in union, in oneness, is there real yoga,
free of all desires and all delusion.
This is the path to liberation.
Doubt will not disappear until you realize oneness within.
If you see something you do not like, you call it madness;
if you like it, you do not see it as madness.
The mind is like a piece of cotton in the wind;
devotion is like water poured on the cotton
so the mind is steadied.
Wetted with the water of wisdom, the consciousness is fixed.
This is liberation.
It is possible to meditate on the Self
even while doing other things;
the objects of the senses are outside us, not inside.
It is possible to keep the buddhi separate.
If the driver of the car takes his hands off the wheel,
the car runs anywhere, there is danger.

Fix the mind in the buddhi, do not let it wander.
Fix it with the practice of inner meditation,
develop the power of introspection.
O mind, enter the sky of consciousness!
Develop the subtle buddhi and fill every nerve of the body.
O mind, be always content - do not be deluded by shadows!*

21   The subtle kundalini shakti must be comprehended
by the path of buddhi.
Like milk being boiled, the prana in the sushumna is heated by
intense faith and discrimination
and led toward the *sahasrara* (still point) in the head.
As the kundalini shakti crosses each chakra,
each guna changes.
The change of one guna means the change of one's whole birth.
As the breath of life, which is in the chakras as
enlightenment, moves upward,
peace and patience flower.
Cross the five chakras, the five houses,
and reach the sixth, the *ajna* chakra, between the eyebrows.
Freed from the six gunas, enter sat-chit-ananda,
being-consciousness-bliss.
Strengthened in the ajna,
enter the fire-circle in the inner heart-sky.
Shiva and Shakti merge and play,
the triple time of past, present, and future merge,
all come together in the bindu.
In the bindu also is the fire of *jnana* (wisdom).
Meditate on this fire.
Attain the *prana-linga*, the seat of consciousness in the head.
Let the prana unite with Shiva and dance as the one Self.
Conquer *mantra* and *yantra*, symbols spoken and drawn.

Let the buddhi rise to the center of the sky of consciousness
and become one with the dawn of the Atman.
Offer up the bodily properties and actions,
let your spirit merge with the absolute Atman.
Seat your spirit at the crest of the sushumna,
which is its real home.
Let the sense of "mine" and "yours" merge,
let all the properties of the individual be unified,
become a *siddha* (perfected one) and be fearless.
Knowing the way to the Absolute, give of this food to others.
Conquer birth and death, be free of birth and death,
enjoy eternal peace.
The light of buddhi reveals all strengths and weaknesses,
all workings of the mind are revealed.
Like the sky and its reflection,
the natural and the subtle are seen separately
by those who have realized the Self.
The inner state is like a jug immersed in water;
all is water.
Be immersed in the waters of wisdom,
let the waters of the Atman wash desires from the mind.
Find joy.
Enter liberation.
Mind, remain always on the path of liberation,
whether walking or sitting, standing or sleeping.
There are no rules of time for liberation.
Even in the midst of crowds,
let your inner being remain in the sky of consciousness.
With intense faith, lead the mind to drink of liberation.
Bhakti and *mukti*, devotion and liberation, are one:
become one with *Omkar*: the power of OM.

22   The fruit is according to inner faith.
Good and evil do not apply to the Self, the Atman.
The Self is like a mirror that reflects the form
the mind creates.
Jiva is like a bird in the nest; when the nest breaks down,
the bird simply flies away.
It may build a new nest in minutes, months, or years.
That depends on its efforts.
From here, you can reach the railway station in an hour
or in a month.

23   Creation dissolves into vayu,
the vital air, blue in color.
Practice raja yoga and experience the bliss
of the indivisible Absolute.
Enter into the One,
dissolve the many.

To bring your Shakti (energy) under control is samadhi.   24
Samadhi is the upward breath, the God within.
When the upward breath is established,
all of the universe is inside you.
The upward breath is the same in all creatures.
The raja yogi is at one with the infinite movement,
whether sitting, talking, standing, or walking.
Raja yoga is like climbing to the roof of a building
and looking around below.
Raja yoga is the highest yoga.
When intellect and wisdom are united, this is raja yoga.
It is complete peace, formless and without qualities.
Bliss has no qualities;
the state without qualities is known as jivanmukti,
Self-Realization.

In raja yoga there are no holy works to be performed.   25
There are no rituals, there is no holiness
in a particular spot or place.
Spiritual discipline consists of
regulating the breath through the chakras.
Respect and love offered from the highest chakra
reach the entire universe.
Creation is nothing but energy
being released or projected from God.
Entering back into it is dissolution.
Identification with the body is the cause of creation
as one sees it.
The real dissolution takes place when
the individual Self merges and dissolves
in the Universal.

26   As air is pumped into a bicycle tire, so the nadis are filled
by thoughts on *Vedanta* (higher knowledge).
First the nadis must be cleansed, then the prana is drawn up,
step by step,
to the Brahmarandhra in the center of the brain.
Merge with the Supreme Self.
Join in the "divine sport."
Mind and intelligence merge into Atman,
intelligence becomes wisdom.
Drink from the well of eternal joy,
penetrate the core of the nectar.
Who is it who is eternally blissful?
Uncover the secret of God's delight.
Awaken the kundalini shakti.
Like a child is rocked to sleep in the cradle,
gather the thoughts in the head
and churn them into a swing.
This is supreme delight, eternal bliss.
Enter into the *Shiva linga* in the head.

Mind, enter the mansion of *ananda* (bliss)! 27
When flood waters cover everything,
the wells and tanks are lost beneath them.
Because of darkness, light is revealed;
when you taste the sweet, remember the pungent.
What is the state of the individual who realizes that
the body is not the Self?
Such a person has regained the original state of purity.
"I" and "mine" are not visible to the physical eye,
they do not exist above the tip of the nose.
That which is above these has no beginning and no end.
All that is seen with the physical eye has both
beginning and end.
The Self is invisible to the physical eye,
it has no beginning and no end.
It is impossible to lessen the power of the Self;
it is ever constant.
The Self is like space, it is the same in all directions.
The head is the abode of light
with the brilliance of millions of suns.
Which is bigger, the eye or the sun?
If the eye is damaged, is it possible to see the sun?
The eye is more important.
The form of images is a creation of the mind.
When a person is photographed
the picture reflects the body of the sitter
not the virtue or lack of virtue of the photographer.

28 Seeing in equality is the upward breath at the time of death.
Equal-sightedness is the divine sight:
indivisible, full of delight, subtle, eternal.
Balancing the incoming and outgoing breaths is yoga;
with the guru's grace, cultivate this balance—
meditate in the head,
meditate on the ocean of eternal delight,
meditate on the ida, the pingala, and the sushumna.
Arise, kundalini-delight!
The match is in the box, the light is in the match;
strike the match and light the fire.
Ignorance is darkness, knowledge is light,
kundalini is the eternal delight.
Kundalini is the eternal delight in the heart,
the "Light of Brahma,"
ablaze with the light of a million suns.
Sunlight is the subtle light,
the solar nerve is the sushumna,
the lunar nerve, the ida, and
the stellar nerve, the pingala.
The essence of the third eye is jnana, wisdom.
In this jnana-nadi there is sleep, *sushupti*;
in sushupti there is no wakefulness.
Balancing the inward and the outward breath,
enjoy the subtle sleep.

Find the eternal joy of the balanced breath.
The seat of the breath is the truth, the inward space,
the chidakash,
unbounded pure awareness, the sky of the heart.
Within the chidakash is the tower of eternal delight,
the seat of peace.
Sleep consciously;
not the gross sleep of the beast, but the sleep of man,
the spiritual sleep,
when talking, when sitting,
without thoughts, without desires, without ideas.
Fix your attention on the breath, listen to the mantra
(sacred sound) of the inward and outward breath.
Do this with bhakti, constant, uninterrupted devotion,
and attain liberation.
Draw the breath up and down, as water is drawn from the well;
puraka is the upward-drawn breath,
kumbhaka is the suspended breath.
Kumbhaka is the "real seat,"
rechaka is the downward breath, the breathing out.
Draw the breath up to the Brahmarandhra, kindle the fire,
purify the nadis,
burn up the impurities.
This is the yoga-fire, the fire of deliberation,
the fire of digestion, the solar light,
the pure energy of the Supreme.
All of the universe is this pure energy.
Creation is but a delusion of the mind;
there is no creation to the equal-sighted.

29 Atman is not perceptible to the physical eye,
it is perceived by the intelligence.
It is not perceptible as something with form or properties;
to those who are identified with the body,
it is difficult to find peace.
It is difficult for them to see the Atman.
Attention towards the visible should be lessened,
attention towards the invisible should be intensified.
As long as the mind dwells on the visible world,
both pain and pleasure are seen,
but in the invisible world
there is neither pain nor pleasure.

30 All rivers ultimately flow into the sea;
all good and all evil merge into the One Self.
All is offered up to the Atman.
Good and evil arise from the Atman;
they return to that from which they came.

When you yourself see the sunrise in the sky of the heart 31
it is possible to describe it.
But you must see it in yourself.
If your mind and intellect are one with the Self,
you can describe it.
If wisdom (jnana) and intelligence are separate,
it is not possible.
What is called "subtle discrimination" is the union of
intelligence and wisdom.
The sun reflected in water is unsteady,
so also the mind is fickle when it is caught in maya.
This is delusion,
this is madness
caused by the gross discrimination;
madness caused by the subtle discrimination is
divine madness.
Whatever you eat, the passage to the stomach is the same.
Whatever the contents of the letter,
the postbox is the same.
It is the tongue that distinguishes
between the sweet and the salt,
to the mind there is no difference.
As you cage the bird and tie its legs
before teaching it to speak,
cage the intelligence in the mind and learn the One.

32 There is no contentment without purification of *chitta*,
consciousness,
no steadiness of mind, no liberation from words
without purification of chitta.
Like ice and water soon become one,
so one who has realized the Atman becomes one with it.
Like rivers merge into the sea,
so desires and impressions merge in the Atman.
Atman is not an object,
karma (force of past action) is an object.
Look at a ship in the sea.
Ship and water appear to be one, but truly they are separate.
Be like the ship in the water:
have no attachment to worldly things.
As the priests wait impatiently for the table to be set
and the meal served,
so you should wait for purification and liberation.

33 Once you have attained perfect peace within,
there is no need to travel anywhere,
there is no need to see anything.
There is no need for pilgrimages to holy places.
All can be seen within.
The coming and going are simply delusions of the mind.
True peace, true liberation is attained
when the one Self in all is seen.
This is liberation from bondage, this is desirelessness.
If you are looking for the object you hold in your hand,
you must look in your hand; it will not be found elsewhere.
So with all things—test them within.

Let the ten senses be restrained in service of the buddhi,   34
like a bird with clipped wings.
Draw the prana from the ten directions into one path,
inward and upward to the heart-sky.
Find inner peace, find liberation in equal-sightedness.
From the heart of freedom, see all as free.
The body is the engine, knowledge is the steam,
discrimination the movement, faith the rail.
Let the train be guided correctly.
Buddhi is the driver, the digestive system is the boiler,
the nadis are the gears.
Enter the Atman through the path of buddhi.
Attain peace.

The Atman is not perceived by the senses;   35
it is distinct and beyond sense-perception.
The Atman is perceived by the organs of knowledge,
by wisdom, by jnana.
It is separate from the body-idea.
Yogis who know the true nature of the senses and
live by that knowledge are *mahatmas*.
What they speak is Veda.
They are like the tamarind seed:
the tamarind fruit is sticky to touch,
but the seed is pure and immaculate.
The heart of the mahatma is like the tamarind seed.
He is eternally young; for him, there is no age-idea.

36   Constant practice is needed to make *vairagya*
(perfect desirelessness) steady and permanent.
Renunciation is not related to the body.
When the mind is fixed and unwavering,
then one sees the Atman.
When both wisdom and divine wisdom have been transcended,
then one sees the Atman.
When one knows but is as if he did not know,
then one sees the Atman.
Those who see the Atman are like blind men though they see,
like the deaf though they hear.
Though they act, it is as if they have not acted.
Even when the senses are functioning,
they are not attached to them,
their actions are like inaction.
Their tendency is greater toward dissolution and
lesser toward creation.
Their capacity to forget is great,
so their actions are inactions.
Their attention is concentrated on the kernel
and not on the shell of the coconut;
on the Atman, not the body.
They are beyond merit and demerit.
They are like a boat in the water; the two are different,
as the gross and the subtle are different.
They are indifferent to the bodily functions,
concentrating only on divine wisdom.
They drink the juice of sugarcane and throw away the rind.
Once the juice is converted to sugar,
it cannot become cane again.
Once the Atman has been realized,
the body-idea never comes back.
As old vessels are renewed by repairs and polish,
when old desires and impressions are tied up and controlled,
buddhi can be transformed into pure illumination.
Then there is contentment.*

Sound arises in akasha, the inner sky.
What manifests in akasha is Life-Power.
What is called akasha is in the head,
the heart-space,
the sky of the heart.
The Life-Power is One.
The difference between the individual and the Universal is like
the difference between the river and the sea;
it is a difference of degree only.
Give up the idea of "I" and "mine."
This idea is the cause of continual rebirth.
To think constantly of "I" and "mine"
is to be of little intelligence.
This is the cause of taking lower birth.
The energy of the sun manifests as light,
the energy of the gas lamp also manifests as light.
To those who have lost the distinction between day and night,
there is no difference between the light of the sun
and the light of the gas lamp.
Faith is the most important thing,
in this world nothing is higher than faith.
Black magic and tricks have no effect
unless you believe in them.
You enjoy that in which you keep your faith.
Concentrate faith on the breath and the thoughts will follow.

38   To repeat *Rama* (a name of God) brings pure delight:
the bliss of the Self,
true and eternal joy,
delight in the inner Self,
kundalini delight.
Rama is the king of mind.
Rama is the essence of the ten senses.
Rama is the Self.
Ravana represents our bad qualities,
Sita is the pure mind,
Lakshmana is persistent concentration,
Krishna is introspection, seeing the Self within.
Seeing the Self within is the eternal inner delight.*

39   Mantra is Brahmarandhra.
Mantra is prime minister of prana,
and this minister of prana is *atma-bindu*
(the spaceless, timeless, causeless point).
In this point is the eternal mantra.
In this point is the chidakash, the sky of consciousness.
This is the supreme joy, the supreme medicine, the supreme guru,
whose mantra is:
That thou art; thou art That.*

Always think of That. 40
Behind the many minds is the one pure Mind.
It is the Mind of All,
It is the eternal Mind.
It is the supreme bliss.
The subtle Mind is the heart-sky, the chidakash,
pure, unbounded consciousness.
The pure Mind is the pure sky;
this is true *siddhi*, attainment,
this is yoga, union with God,
this is the heart.
Fulfillment is possible only when you merge in this pure heart;
there, all idea of "you" and "I" disappears.
In the chidakash is liberation, shakti, love and devotion.
Buddhi (intelligence) is in the chidakash.
When you live in the chidakash, all attachments burn away.
The pure sky is Brahmarandhra.

What is called akasha is in the upward direction. 41
What is called male is a subtle state,
what is called female is dynamic.

42	The search for truth requires subtle discrimination.
The subtle is merged in the gross.
The seat of discrimination is in the sky of the heart.
When the kundalini is raised to the heart-space in the head,
then the breath is single,
the universe is in one's Self.
All is in the Atman;
creation, dissolution—all forms, all events—
are seen in One.
To see separateness is hell; to see unity is liberation.
Absolute love and devotion are liberation.
Complete peace, endless peace, is the goal—
Yogananda, Paramananda.
The ocean is greater than all the rivers.
The ocean has no limits.
The ocean's water cannot be measured.
It is not possible to cultivate love and devotion by giving up
samsara (the cycle of worldly existence).
Remain in samsara and attain liberation
by being "this thing" and doing "that thing."
Desire is samsara; liberation is desirelessness.
Eternal bliss, the joy of being and knowledge,
the Self, God, One;
all are the same.
The highest state is boundless peace,
liberation is eternal bliss,
love and devotion are the state of sat-chit-ananda.*

Upanayana (inner initiation) is the true fulfillment; 43
"upa" means "to dwell near."
The individual must be merged in the Divine.
The real upanayana is internal, subtle.
The subtle discrimination is the third eye.
Fulfillment is to be near God.
Upanayana is not for the body, but beyond,
to the thought of the Self.
He who has performed such discrimination is a *brahmin* (priest).
Subtle discrimination is the sushumna,
it is the nadi of God, where gods and goddesses dwell.

One who has not realized the truth 44
is a beggar.
One who has not destroyed delusion,
who has not left the worldly path
is a beggar.

45   The body is the soul's nest, the soul's house.
To distinguish "this house" and "that house"
is subtle discrimination.
The house of the gross body is a beggarly house.
What can be said about Brahmananda!
Who can describe it?
Truly, truly know that the eternal is One in all.
Hari is not the knower, Shiva is the knower.
Hari is wandering, Hari is demanding:
"Hari, I want this!"
"I want that!"
"Give me, give me!"
This is useless, it does not bring happiness.
Let Hari merge in Hara; burn Hari in Hara.
Crying "Hari, Hari" is mental delusion.
Turn from delusion, turn within.
Shiva is the giver of eternal delight.
Shiva is the giver of eternal liberty and devotion.
Hari is keeping the mind in the world,
Shiva is keeping the universe within.
Hari is the downward path,
Shiva is the guide to the path of bliss,
the upward path of liberation.
Hari is like a horse without reins.*

The fragrances of musk, sandal-paste, and camphor are 46
experienced in the head.
Ants swarm where there is sugar.
Where the sound of OM is experienced there is no ignorance.
The spiritual eye, not the physical eye, sees the real heart.
The head is the highest.
The origin of breath is *nijananda*: real bliss.
Real bliss is in the cave of the heart.
The house of breath is the dwelling place of kundalini,
the house of Shiva,
house of fulfillment,
house of balance and harmony.
One who lives in this house
does not care about honor or dishonor.
This is the home of the yogi who has renounced everything.
It is the home of the subtle discrimination,
the home of kundalini, the home within the heart.

Those whose minds are pure may call God by any name. 47
Experience is the train, wisdom is the passenger,
the chakras are the stations.
The subtle is in the chakras, in the subtle tube.
Within the subtle tube is the kundalini shakti,
the kundalini shakti and the subtle tube are OM.
Realize and know the subtle.

PART TWO
BUDDHI

BUDDHI

Achutamama was a great devotee from the earliest days in Udipi; he followed Nityananda everywhere. One day in 1920, some local scholars were holding a symposium on metaphysics. One of the pundits had a great intuitive respect for Nityananda and therefore invited him to attend, even though on a strictly scholastic basis, he would not have been asked. Nityananda took his faithful, but practically illiterate, devotee with him. They both listened to the discussions and eventually Nityananda was asked to say a few words. He immediately turned to his unfortunate companion and prodded him to rise and speak. Achutamama was totally taken aback and even a little angry, thinking that it was not fair of the Master to play such a cruel joke on him. But the prodding went on and finally he had no choice but to rise. At once he found words were coming from him. He did not know what he spoke, but it must have been acceptable, as he finished to smiles and applause from the assembly!

In 1916 as some villagers were crossing the railroad tracks north of Pandalaquin Railway Station, one of the men had a seizure. He fell on the tracks and froth came out of his mouth. No one knew what to do; soon a helpless crowd had gathered. Suddenly a thin, dark-skinned young man appeared in their midst, smiling calmly. He put some *vibhuti* ash (miraculously manifested) in the dying man's mouth and instantly it was as if nothing had ever happened to him: the man stood up completely cured. The dark young man ignored the growing crowd and simply sat down on the tracks. As the excited crowd continued to grow, someone called out that he was none other than Ishwar Iyer's Nityananda.

Soon the railroad authorities appeared, annoyed by the large crowd near the tracks. The local sub-inspector had such a reputation for terrorizing the poor railway coolies that he was nicknamed "Kaduva," or "Tiger." This man had taken up the unfortunately common English attitude that looked contemptuously at native Indian culture and spirituality. Thus, when he saw the large crowd gathered around the silent, dark young man, he stormed into the crowd and shouted abuse at Nityananda, threatening to kill him if he came near the station. But Nityananda simply smiled and moved a little further down the tracks; it was as if he had not heard the "Tiger" at all.

Soon it was time for the Madras/Mangalore Express to arrive. The "Tiger" directed the Anglo-Indian driver to continue at full speed; let the mad man be crushed if he would not listen. But to every one's great surprise, Nityananda burst into gales of laughter and the massive engine came to a grinding halt. All the efforts of the engineer notwithstanding, the train would not budge a single inch.

Like a huge tree felled, the "Tiger" fell at the feet of the smiling Nityananda and begged his pardon. Demonstrating his major change of heart, the railway man constructed a small ashram for Bhagavan at the village of Kothamangalam, where Nityananda stayed for three days. On the third night, he left.

The Sutras

In the Indivisible, there is no divisible.   48
For the *jnani* (one who has realized the Self),
there is no ignorance.
For the ignorant, there is no wisdom.
A mother loves all her children equally;
even if they trouble and beat her,
she does not cast them out.
The jnani loves all equally.

49 A jnani has no mind,
he sees all things equally.
He is beyond the three states of sleep, dream, and deep sleep.
For him there is no sunrise or sunset.
When the glass chimney of a lamp is covered with soot,
light is not reflected clearly.
The soot of ignorance must be removed from the mind,
so it may clearly reflect
the light of the Atman within.*

50 The true jnani
renounces worldly pleasures
and by practicing yoga
experiences complete union with the divine force within.
Bliss does not come from listening,
it can only be experienced.
One who has experienced divine bliss is a mahatma.
It is not by seeing stone and earth
that one becomes a mahatma,
only one who sees the Self in himself is a mahatma.

The essential knowledge must be attained by everyone.   51
What is this essential knowledge?
For the individual Self to know
the mystery of the universal Self.

One who doesn't know the true goal of human life   52
is just an animal.
The true goal is wisdom.
One who doesn't know this is not a true man.
Human life is the highest in creation;
it must not be spent like the frog in the water,
rising and sinking
rising and sinking
again and again and again.
Human life is the highest in creation,
it cannot always be attained.
When the opportunity is there, work towards the goal.
First cook, then eat.
Discrimination is the fire, intelligence the vessel,
mukti the goal.

53   The head is the ocean of delight, the seat of bliss,
the thousand-petalled lotus,
the seat of liberation.
This knowledge is not found in books,
it is inherent in the brain.
Books are made of parts,
but the jnana (knowledge) that shines in the head
is one undivided whole.
A book has many chapters, but jnana is single-chaptered.
Books are for those who are not established in jnana.
For the person with realization,
knowledge is stable, eternal, and indivisible.
A person is born with a brain, not a book.
At the moment of death, there is no book.
Only in the middle do you take up a book.*

54   No one criticizes the king to his face,
but behind his back, they criticize him.
Worldly people dare not criticize the jnani directly.
If you enter a dark room after being in the bright sun
you see nothing.
When you emerge from the dark into the light,
You cannot know whence you have come.

Birds are like airplanes. 55
Men are like animals.
Animals are like men.
Dogs are like jnanis.
Feed a dog once and it will not forget till it dies.
It will have constant love for the master
who fed it only once.
Ordinary men have no subtle discrimination;
they don't know where they have come from, and
they don't know where they are going.
But a man of perfect understanding has
constant love and devotion.

The gross state is of the mind, 56
the subtle state is of the Atman.
The jnani is always in *yoga-nidra*, yoga-sleep,
whether walking or sitting.
He is like the tortoise:
he projects his arms and legs only when they are needed.
At other times, they are withdrawn into the shell.

57 A man whose mind is merged in samadhi is not deluded
by the external magic show.
He fears nothing, to him there is no fear in the world.
In his presence even the tiger and the cobra
forget their aggressiveness.
All creatures become calm.
Even enemies forget their hostility and become quiet.
Why?
Because of the doubt.
There is no darkness then;
the mind is purified by the *sattva guna*, pure light.

58 Just as the mind of a person carrying a burden on his head
is concentrating on balancing it there,
just as the actor playing the king
keeps his concentration on the crown,
so the attention of the jnani is concentrated on buddhi.

Fill the lamp with oil and light the wick.   59
As the oil is used up and the wick shortens, the light dims.
If the oil is replenished and the wick is set,
the lamp shines as before.
The inner life of the jnani is similar,
it is like butter put in water.
The butter does not sink to the bottom,
but floats above the water.
The body is the water, the spirit is the butter.
The subtle intelligence must be placed in the head,
the buddhi should be at the top of the sushumna.
Both mind and buddhi should be in the head.
Mind in the head, mind in the buddhi, buddhi in the mind.
Discrimination comes from buddhi;
from discrimination comes the union of jiva with the Self.

In a house without lamp-light   60
there is no hospitality or warmth.
In that house people bump into each other and the furniture.
The lamp is wisdom,
the light is kundalini.

61   If you have mind, you want everything;
if you have no mind, you want nothing.
If you have mind, then "god" is seen as a separate being.
When mind is merged in buddhi, no separate god is needed;
all is seen as One.
If you have desires, a god is needed to fulfill them.
Then, mind chases the objects of the senses; doubt arises,
leading to a need for an image to worship.
Cause and effect appear to be separate.
This is delusion and ignorance.

62   After you have learned to write on paper,
there is no need to revert to
writing in sand spread on the floor.
After you have attained knowledge of the *nirguna* state,
the state of the Absolute without name, form, or attributes,
there is no need to study its many forms.
Can the curds be changed back to milk?

Before their brains develop, babies see no difference 63
in the world around them.
It is only when their brains develop
that the sense of difference develops.
Until a baby is six months old, he knows no difference.
A true yogi is like such a young baby.
If you gave the baby a diamond, he would throw it away;
to him, a rock and a diamond are the same.
Similarly, to a true jnani,
a lump of earth and money are the same.
He is not attached to either one.
All is the Self; he sees the Self in all and all in the Self.
This is the inner vision, the subtle thought.
The subtle thought is Shiva-Shakti.
Shiva-Shakti is the Shakti of the indivisible Parabrahma,
and Parabrahma Shakti is the Self.
This is the One reality.

64   Where water flows, there is no mud. Mud is **ignorance**,
devotion and wisdom are the water.

65   When a speck of dust blows into your eye,
all of your attention turns to it.
Turn the attention inward, this is the inner sight.
Ignorance is like a box filled with dust.
Only the person who filled the box knows its contents,
no one else knows.
The power and energy of life are the real wealth,
buddhi is the box.
Place the wealth in the box and lock it.
Now the mind is in its proper place in the head.
It is man's duty to return the treasure he has been given,
the treasure of the Self.
Return to the Self within, know your own secret,
the universe is inside you, you are inside the universe.
The inner Self is the One who dances in all,
the One who is here and the One who is there.

The supreme light is also the universal light.   66
O mind, discard the idea of "otherness" and
hold the idea of "sameness."
You were born with breath; when you depart,
you leave only breath.
This body of earth is not made or taken away.
The gift of Shiva is the same for all,
all seeds have the same power in them,
the subtle in all seeds is One,
the difference is in behavior only.
The delusions of the mind are not permanent.
All that is seen and heard is temporary.

Doubtlessness is the path to one-pointedness of mind.   67
The intelligence of a doubting person dwindles;
wherever he looks, he sees nothing but doubt.
Everyone is subject to his own nature.
There is no reason to find qualities
that are not in your own nature.
You cannot see your reflection in agitated water;
in still water, the reflection can be seen properly.
To a fickle-minded man, his real nature is not visible;
for the man with steady mind, everywhere he looks,
he sees the One, indivisible.
He sees himself in others.
Through red glasses, everything appears red, not green.
Everyone sees according to his thinking.

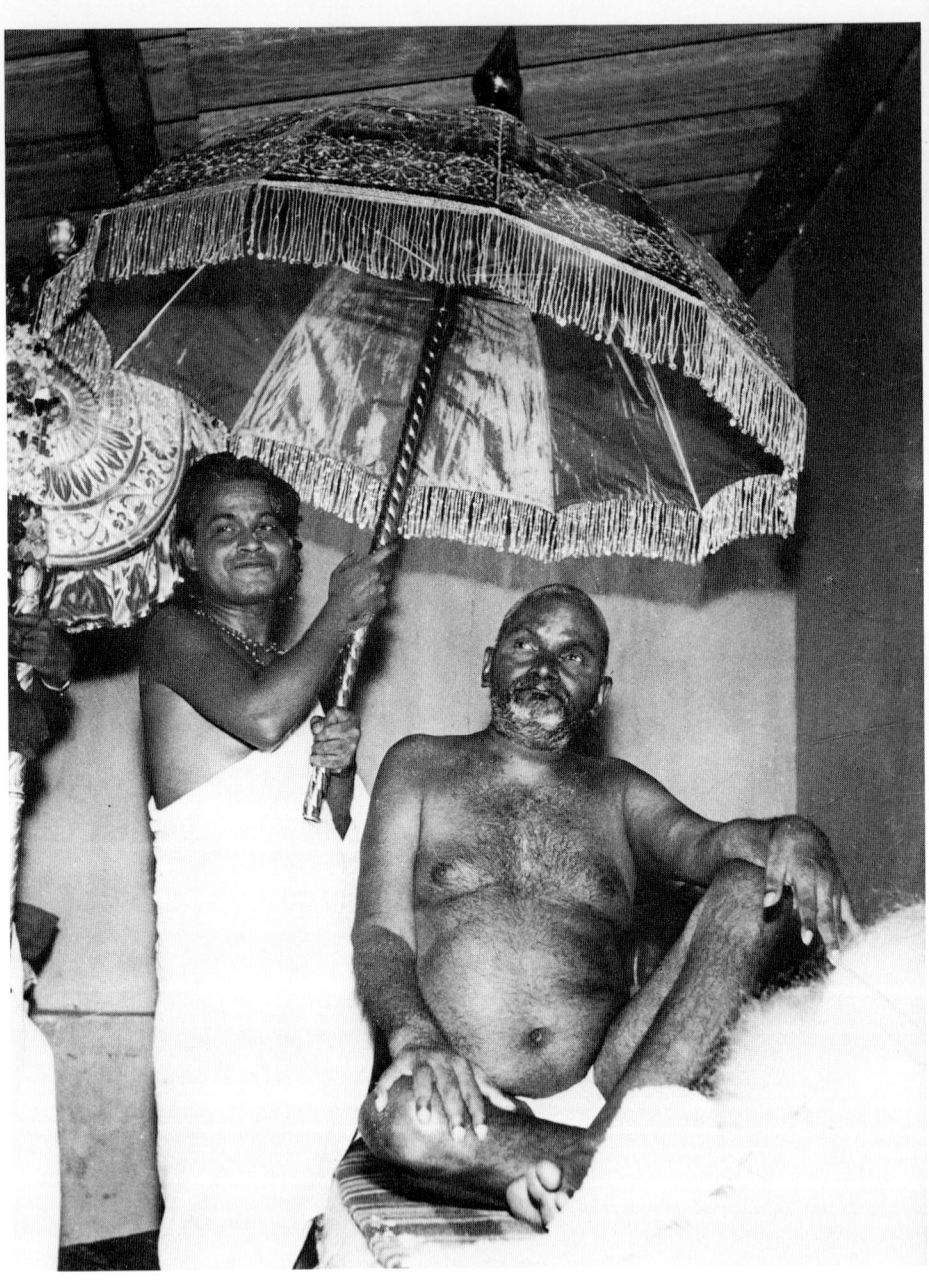

Nityananda with Shaligram Swami, whose samadhi shrine is also at Ganeshpuri

The well must be emptied of water 68
and cleansed of accumulated mud.
Then the pure water of the spring can flow freely.
Divine wisdom is like the pure water.
Burn away the accumulated thoughts of "I" and "mine,"
then true knowledge will pour forth in its simple purity.

In deep sleep there is no mind. 69
In deep sleep, you are near the Self.
In the states of waking, dreaming, and thought-play,
you are deceived into a sense of active participation.
Remember that this is not real.
Merge the knowledge of the Unseen with the Seen
and find perfect bliss.
Only one who has attained such knowledge is a
Swami, Yogi, and Guru.

70 When the life-energy moves in an outward direction,
desires are born.
There follows the mind, which divides and subdivides
into the two-, four-, and six-fold gunas, and
what is called "the world" comes into being.
All other gunas arise from this beginning.
Once born, the organs of knowledge are the most needed by man.
The five organs of action relate to the earth,
this is the *Sad-guna*.
The five organs of knowledge relate to the gross akasha,
this is the *Chid-guna*.
He who conquers the senses is a free man; for him,
fulfillment arises from within.

71 Mind is the root of bondage and liberation,
of good and evil, of sin and holiness.
The mind creates thought, which leads to actions, and finally,
to results.
If there is no mind, there is no speech,
no coming and no going.
Nothing is done.
In school, to speak English without knowing writing
is not enough. Both must be known, then alone can one pass.

Why is man called man?   72
A true man is a person who thinks and reflects.
Ignorance of the path to Self leads to rebirth
again and again.
If you do not know this path, you will find no contentment.
Contentment comes from knowing the path of spirituality and
from doing your work without attachment to its results.
This is desirelessness, liberation, the supreme delight.
Desire is hell.
Desirelessness is the supreme joy.
The highest state is Shiva-Shakti,
Shiva-Shakti is the experience of the Here and the Beyond.

In the beginning, mind and Self are the same to all people.   73
At the end, in the state of universal dissolution,
it is also the same.
Only in the interval
of breathing, thinking, and actions
is there difference.

74 Dharana (perfect concentration) is the means
for buddhi to increase its power of understanding.
Dharana is a path to liberation, a path to the highest.
Dharana is a means to steady the breath of Life (*prana-vayu*),
and when the prana-vayu is steady, the mind becomes steady.
When the prana is turned upward,
divine wisdom enters every nerve;
peace is the result.
Then nature and the subtle are separate,
then the buddhi can experience
yoga-power, peace, forgiveness, contentment.
If you practice this concentration,
you will find the whole world within.
The mind so steadied enjoys eternal bliss.
The Self is beyond all karma.
True karma is work done without attachment to its fruits.
There is no sin without the sense of doing.
True karma is work done in the knowledge of the Self,
which is actionless and passionless.

A lamp cannot burn without oil, 75
the body cannot function without breath,
without a rudder, a boat cannot be steered to harbor.
A steamship is guided by steam power and the skill of the captain,
a country boat cannot go like a steamship.
The sannyasi is like the steamship;
he who has put the world inside himself is like the steamship.
The man who is in the world is like the country boat.
The Brahmarandhra of the sannyasi is like the guiding light
atop the steamship.
The mind of the sannyasi is merged in the hridayakasha,
the light is the sannyasi.
The cow cannot run like the horse.
A person whose mind is merged in the Self is like the horse,
one whose mind is in the world is like the cow.
Everyone cannot be king at once,
everyone cannot be traders at once;
customers are also required.

76   The seeds of the mind,
when fed into the mill of spiritual discernment,
produce the oil of "wisdom-nectar."

77   Without deep faith there can be no desirelessness.
When mind is dissolved, there can be no desire.
Without faith, there are no fruits.
It is the mind's delusion that pays thousands for a diamond;
without mind, diamonds are nothing but lumps of earth.

The selfish mind is not firm and steady,   78
subtle discrimination alone is steady.
Creation is peace,
creation is the Witness,
creation is subtle discrimination.
This discrimination gives nourishment, gives liberation.
Yukti (cleverness) is not superior to Shakti,
Shakti contains yukti,
yukti is a modification of the mind.
The real intelligence is subtle discrimination.
True Shakti is subtle discrimination.

No one is mad in this world.*   79

80   A man without desire has no need of a separate god,
he does not need to strive for anything.
When the mind runs after desires,
striving is necessary to bring the mind to one-pointedness.
Concentrate the mind in the buddhi
as long as the pulse beats,
as often as the pulse beats.
Do not unite the mind with the senses.
Whatever you do, keep the inner state aloof.
One sinking under water must learn to swim above it.
Conquer maya (delusion) with conscious effort.
Because of maya you experience different states
as your mind runs into various objects.
You cling to the coconut tree,
the coconut tree does not cling to you.
Does maya have arms and legs to seize you?

81   As camphor is consumed in fire,
so the mind must be consumed in the Self.
The moment camphor catches fire, it is transformed into fire
and burns itself out of existence,
leaving no trace behind.
When mind merges in the Self no trace of ego remains.

As water is contained in a reservoir, 82
so the mind must be contained.
It must not get out of control
like swollen rivers during monsoon.
Mind is the cause of both good and evil;
"good" and "evil" are ideas of the mind,
God does neither good nor evil.
Knowledge and wisdom come from the Divine;
take the protection of divine wisdom's armor.
Not even a bullet can pierce it.

The umbrella does not hold you, 83
all is held by the mind.
When the moods of the mind are conquered,
all difference disappears.
Such a person has no desire; he is a sannyasi, he is a yogi.
A person with mind wants everything,
the person with no mind has everything inside.
Just as a steamship carries all things needed for the journey,
so the person who has overcome mind
carries the universe within him.

84   Subtle intellect is the jnana of buddhi.
Inner concentration is one-pointed.
The gross intellect is like the horse unreined;
it is not steady,
it is not permanent,
it is not Hari,
it is not Shiva.
Knowledge from the guru is subtle intelligence, not gross.
Gross intelligence is the intelligence of animals.
He is no man who does not return what he has been given.

85 It is the mind that observes *mouna*,(silence) not the tongue.
Whatever is done when intelligence and wisdom
are united in the Self is not karma.
Silence is native to the mind, not the tongue.
Sadhana (spiritual practice; pursuit of an ideal)
is done by mouna.
A yogi has united intelligence and wisdom.
He places the mind in buddhi and under control of buddhi.
Of the nadis, three are most important:
the ida, pingala, and sushumna.
Sushumna is the seat of kundalini.
The discipline of silence is really the Brahmarandhra,
the junction of the ida, pingala, and sushumna nadis.*

A person who has given up all sense of honor or dishonor   86
is filled with bliss, true bliss,
Brahmananda: union with the Absolute.
If the workings of the mind and intellect are concentrated
for even five minutes,
everything becomes That.
Those who do not recognize the universal Cause
do not understand the purpose of life.
Like moths they are attracted to the fatal flame,
they are caught in maya's net of delusion.
Like moths, they live in view of the flame,
playing in and around it
only to fall in at last and perish.

PART THREE
OMKAR

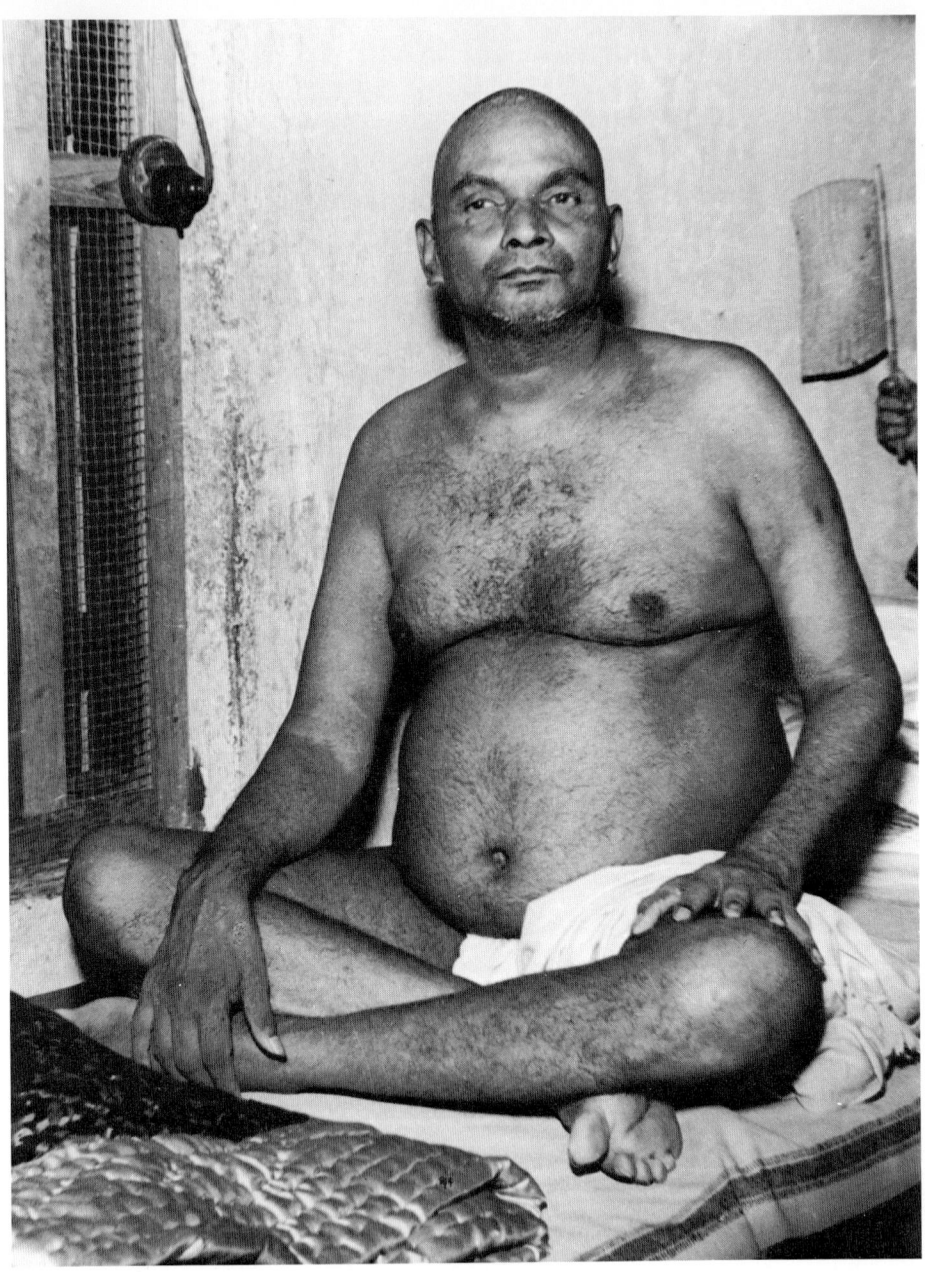

OMKAR

Nityananda was always totally immersed in the Divine, in Omkar. A devotee from the South Kanara years, known as Achutamama, recalls the following incident. Near the coastal village of Kaup there was a lighthouse under the charge of an English caretaker who admired Nityananda and made him welcome at the lighthouse whenever he wished to come. One night, Nityananda took Achutamama to the top of the lighthouse. Pointing out a large ship lying at anchor in the distance, Nityananda asked his companion to estimate the depth of the sea at the ship. To the answer, "Must be quite deep for a ship like that," the youthful Nityananda replied, "Oh, no! It is only ankle deep. Come, I will show you."

It was a dark night. As soon as they got into the sea, Nityananda took his devotee's arm with his right hand and stretched his left hand out in front of them. They walked in ankle-deep water all the way to the side of the ship. The bewildered Achutamama did not understand and could not answer when Nityananda told him, "See, it is only ankle-deep as you were told." They turned around and walked back as they had come, Nityananda again holding his companion with one hand while he held the other arm stretched out. Halfway to shore, Nityananda lowered his outstretched hand; both men immediately sank into the deep sea. Achutamama was terrified, but in seconds, Nityananda had reached him and pulled him up. Again they started walking through ankle-deep water, with

Nityananda's left hand outstretched as before. Upon returning to the room where they were to spend the night, the exhausted Achutamama immediately fell into a deep sleep. He awoke at about midnight. Nityananda was sitting up looking at him; seeing that his companion was awake, Nityananda began to speak. He said that what had happened was a manifestation of the Omkar Shakti, and that everything in the universe was a manifestation of this Omkar. As soon as he had heard these two sentences, Achutamama fell back into his deep sleep.

Whenever devotees would begin to tell their tales of woe, Nityananda would wave them aside, saying: "Everything is known; did the Pandavas moan to Krishna about their difficulties? Was he not aware of them?"

A young wife in Mangalore was often reprimanded by her husband for her devotion to Nityananda, or for visiting places where he was found; once in a rage over her disobedience he lashed her with a belt until blood was drawn. Days later, the devotee had a chance to see Nityananda and she immediately told him of her plight. The Master replied: "You got the lash but who got the pain? See?" He showed her his back, and indeed, the marks of the lashing were there.

Another woman, pure, simple, and very devout, visited Nityananda in the mid-fifties and recounted some worries of her own. Nityananda shook his head: "Have you not yet understood who this one is? Are you not convinced of this place? Still worrying? Have faith and conviction. Everything will happen in its time."

The Sutras

Omkar (the power of OM) is One, the universal force.   87
In OM is creation
and the dissolution of creation.
In OM is the dissolution of mind.
Omkar is Atman, the eternal Self in you.
OM is indivisible; that which can be divided is not the whole.
From the beginning there is only one truth revealed by God.
When you sit inside a closed room,
you are not aware of any "outside."
When the doors are shut,
jivatman and paramatman are one.
When the doors are opened, mind separates from Omkar;
jivatman and paramatman also appear distinct.

88
All is He, the One pervading all,
the One beyond all qualities.
He is One, He is OM.
His form is everlasting peace.
He blesses those who trust in him and
punishes those who ridicule.
He eases the time of death for devotees.
O God, turn me from the downward path and
show me the middle way.
The giver is Shiva.

89
All things are forms of Omkar.
Omkar is the divine in them,
Omkar is the subtle bindu.
As the vital air, Omkar pervades all things, inner and outer.
It is impossible to describe Shiva-Shakti.
Only if you have experienced it yourself can you describe it.
Without the experience,
it is impossible to say what Shiva-Shakti is.
Book knowledge is of no help in describing it.
But a person with experience of the Self
can describe it.

God manifests in the form of peace.   90
OM is the form of peace.
He is without form, without change.
He is above discrimination, Absolute.
Like children rocked to sleep in the cradle,
with mind as the pillow, sleep inwardly.

The Self resides in the cave of the body.   91
Freedom from the bondage of duality is the highest goal.
The physical body has many different parts,
the power that creates and sustains it is One and indivisible.
Omkar pervades the entire universe,
pranava (the resonance of Omkar) pervades the form.
OM has neither form nor shape.

92   Does sound arise from the universe or
does the universe arise from sound?
Effect from cause or cause from effect?
The universe arises from sound;
from sound, form arises, and all things that have form.
From the cause is the effect.
But how does the cause arise?
Both cause and effect are in the Self,
both cause and effect are to serve one's Self,
both cause and effect arise from the Self.
In the Self, cause and effect merge into One.
The delusion that arises in the Self subsides into the Self.
A lie is a lie.
If you believe a lie, then you must speak the lie.
If you believe the truth, then you must speak the truth.
Those who speak falsely have no truth in them;
there is no falsehood separate from them,
falsehood is one with them.
What is the cause of falsehood?
They become so accustomed to it
that it no longer looks like falsehood to them,
they are not aware of any separate thing called "falsehood."
If they do recognize falsehood as a separate thing,
then they will no longer incline to it;
they will look for the good, they will find the right path.

The subtle state, the omnipresent universal force, 93
is the same in everything, and is the same everywhere.
There is no distinction between the moving and the still.
There is difference only in causation; difference is delusion,
difference is in the body.
The body is transient,
to see the subtle in the gross is liberation.
Liberation is indivisible.
Liberation is in the sky of the heart.
In the heart is the Shiva linga,
self-existence,
the chief prana,
the upward breath,
the prana-vayu.
The prana is the One, it is the One in all.
To those who practice and see, it is One.
For those who do not practice,
there is only the bondage of desire.
Withdraw the desires and attain liberation in this life.
Realize the One principle,
turn the eye inward and see the truth.
One who has turned the mind inward is the true *Purusha*;
the universe is in him and he is in the universe.
The mind, when involved in the world, cannot be steady.
The Shiva in the heart is steady, is One,
is Omkar.
Omkar united with forms is pranava.
Omkar is the "disassociation" of the bodily awareness.

94 Omkar is all-pervading;
like the dawn of the sun, OMkar is the witness of all things.
Omkar is the most frightful of all forms,
Omkar is fire (*agni*).
There is nothing greater than fire, all is fire
both within and without.
Earth is in the middle,
above is air, vayu. Air is in the universe,
the universe is in the air.
Air is first, fire second. Thought is first, sound is second.
Soundlessness is in the form of air.
Soundlessness is eternal delight.
It is sat-chit-ananda: being-knowledge-delight.
Merge your Self in soundlessness.
All the visible universe is in the Self.
When chit and sat are merged, there is bliss, joy, delight,
the delight of discrimination, *vivekananda*,
the delight of consciousness, *chaitanyananda*,
the delight of Brahman, *Brahmananda*,
the delight of the Supreme, *paramananda*,
the eternal delight, *nityananda*, and
the delight of being and consciousness, *sat-chit-ananda*.
This is true adulthood, this is wisdom,
the wisdom of God, the wisdom of yoga, the wisdom of time.
The "three time wisdom" is in the heart.
Liberation is in the heart.
Eternal bliss is in the heart.

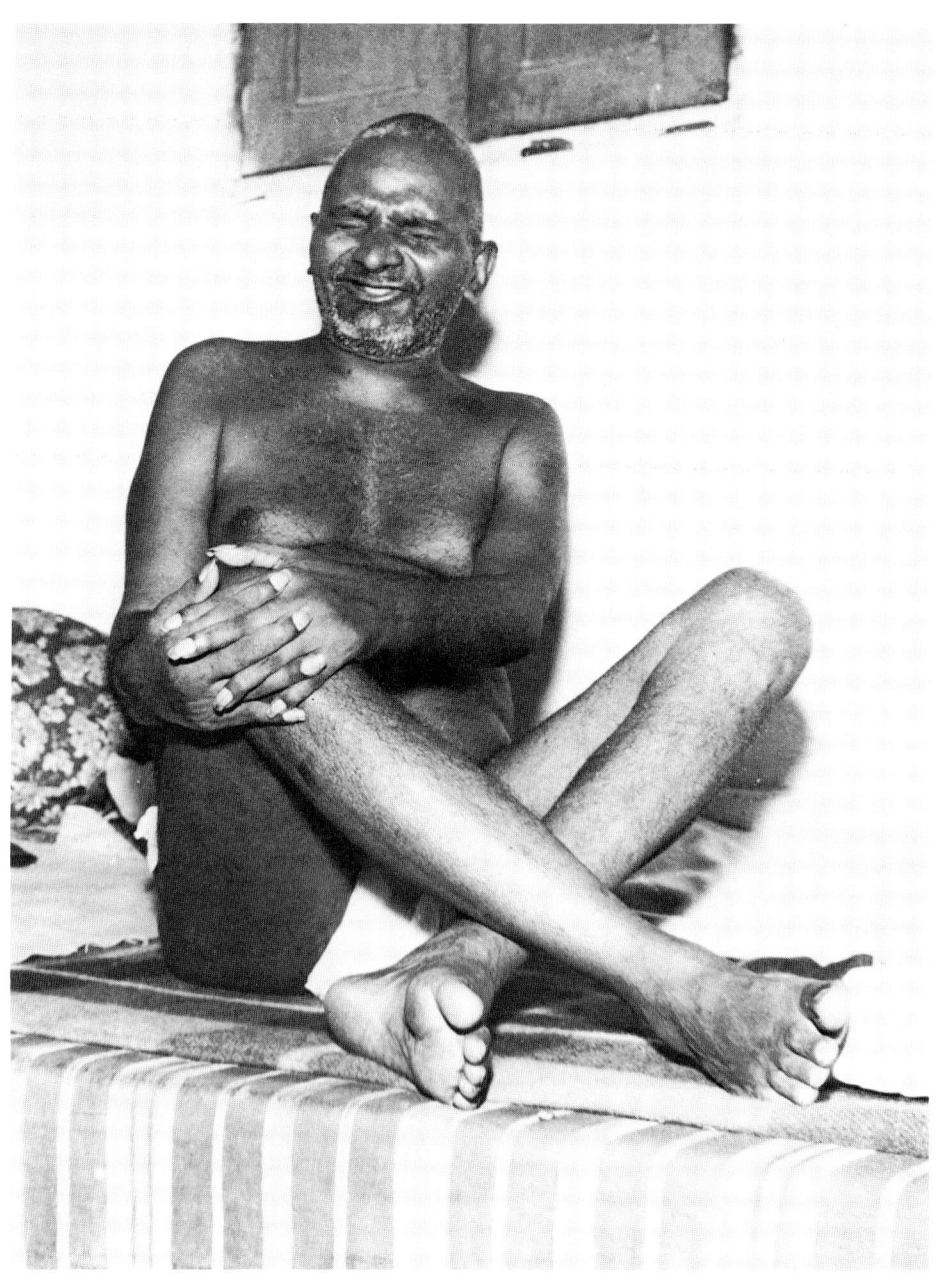

Nityananda in Kailas, the second ashram building at Ganeshpuri, occupied in 1956.

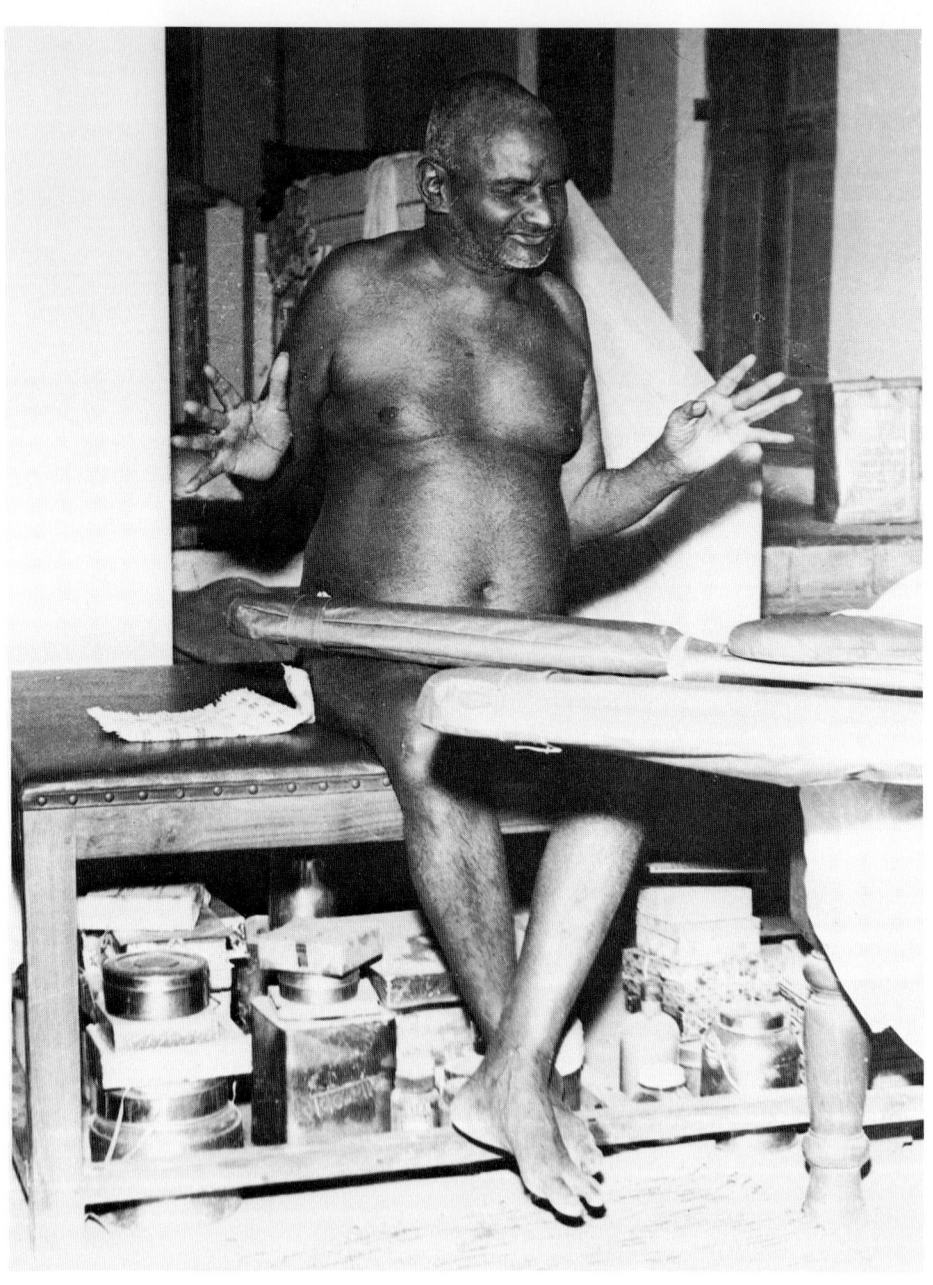

Nityananda in Kailas. The special darshan chair with extensions is also visible.

The OM-sound vibrates like a storm in the sky.
It has neither beginning nor end.
It is the stage manager of the divine drama.
The body of man is a string of OM, it is filled with OM.
All that is, inside us, outside us,
everywhere,
is born of OM.
We do not need to search for it,
it is present in everything.
No special effort is needed to recall it to memory.
The Shakti that is the OM-sound is not finite,
it is infinite and indivisible.
It exists in all creatures.
The sound produced by any creature is nothing but OM.
Pranava is OM.
When OM unites with prana and moves in the body,
this is pranava.
When nature and the subtle are separate, it is pranava;
when both are felt to be one, there is the Oneness,
OM.
OM is seen everywhere.
Wherever you place your faith, that becomes All.
The Shakti that is OM fills and penetrates the universe,
it is formless,
it is the light in all directions.
Ignorance and knowledge are not real,
neither pain nor pleasure has effect.

95

96   The energy of the OM-sound is like an infinite ocean,
it moves in all directions, it pervades all,
both inside and outside.
In the form of buddhi
it becomes creation, preservation, dissolution;
it becomes soundless.
The unstruck sound merges in buddhi.
Buddhi dissolves in the OM-sound,
all merge and become one.
OM and reason,
the world and buddhi,
the world and OM merge into the heart-sky,
the heart-sky merges into buddhi,
buddhi into akasha,
akasha and buddhi into Omkar,
the imperishable and buddhi merge.
Wisdom and the imperishable merge into buddhi,
buddhi and the Self,
the Self into buddhi,
all thoughts of Form into Self through buddhi,
cause and effect into Self.
Knowledge and ignorance become one with the Self
through the path of buddhi.
Peace is as pure as the sky of consciousness,
a deep purity beyond the distinctions of pure/impure,
eternally pure,
formless and changeless.
In peace, form and change unite with buddhi and
expand infinitely in all directions, through all things,
eternally equal.
Peace has no purpose, no motive;
it should never be associated with motive.
It is quite separate.
It is the highest state.

By the path of buddhi,
peace is neither of this world nor of the next.
It is not touched by either pleasure or pain.
The understanding that there is one Atman in all
is true peace; peace that gives happiness both Here and There.
This is the word of Veda, the *dharma* (law) of the holy,
the fulfillment of human birth.
It is liberation, the fulfillment of human birth.
It is Truth, it is the highest state, it is All.
It is desireless devotion, *nishkama bhakti*.
Nishkama bhakti is complete absence of desire
and this desirelessness is freedom from cares,
which is the true state of the Self.
O mind, give up your desire for this thing and that thing.
Serve the Self, serve the Truth.
Delight in the inner play of the Self,
delight in sat-chit-ananda.
Forget day and night, be forever in the light of buddhi.
See the entire universe as nothing but the Self.
Let the Self encompass the three states of
waking, sleep, and deep sleep.
Cultivate *maha-shanti* (the great peace) in the Self,
sing its glory to all the universe.
Mind will understand Truth through the intelligence.
Truth is not a religion, Truth cannot be taught.
You must discover it in your own Self,
and then let it expand in OM.
Sacrifice memory to buddhi,
thoroughly quiet the consciousness (chitta),
let Truth alone remain.
Merge Truth in the chidakash,
be one with the sky of consciousness.
See the universe with equal vision.
Realizing equal vision, dissolve the sense of "you" and "I";
recognize Truth with this same-sightedness.
There is nothing other than Truth:
this is the state of sat-chit-ananda.
Truth is the beginning and the end, inside and outside;
Truth is One.

Establish this Truth of oneness in your heart
through concentration and understanding;
this is the highest state.
Truth is sugar, the juice of fruit that grows on
the tree of desirelessness.
This is the sweet juice of wisdom, it is the juice of yoga
that transforms every quality (guna) of the body.
Direct it upward,
shake off all doubts by bathing in the waters of Shiva,
let Shiva and Shakti unite with OM.
Look at the forms and properties of the world
with the third eye,
burn all doubts to ashes, burn the six enemies to ashes,
cover yourself with these ashes and join Shiva.
Enter the third eye.
Be thou Shiva and Shiva, thou.
Do not hesitate to sacrifice the difference
between you and Shiva;
throw it into the fire of the five senses.
Sacrifice all doubts in these fires, sacrifice all qualities.
Established in desirelessness, drink the nectar every moment,
drink freely.
When you know Truth, there is no fear of death.
"I" and "mine" are dissolved,
"I" and "mine" are nothing but fear of death.
This is an obstruction on the path to God.
When you know Truth, death is just an external condition,
like sleep.
In Truth there is no distinction between inner and outer;
when the senses are turned inward,
"I" and "mine" dwindle to nothing.
Only when you waken from sleep and
become aware of the external
do you understand the nature of sleep.
So also with wisdom.
Birth and death are caused by desire,
desire turns the shadow to reality.
This desire is under your control.

In the discrimination of buddhi,
fear of birth and death disappears.
When the mind is subject to desire,
you experience pleasure and pain, you need external help.
When desire is controlled,
pleasure and pain have no influence.
If you become the slave of habits,
you will take a lower birth.
Habits must be controlled, you must exercise the will.
Any work done on a whim is temporary,
but work done by exercise of the buddhi is life-long.
Whims or fancies are never permanent,
they are much inferior to buddhi;
they are like the little finger and
buddhi like the middle finger.
Great attachment to some particular thing creates *vasanas*;
(tendencies carried from life to life),
and these vasanas are the cause of rebirth.
Vasanas that relate to the body come and go
like bubbles on the water,
but great attachments create vasanas that cause another birth.
These vasanas have a special form that reflects the internal.
For a man with such a vasana, whatever work he may do,
it is only the body working.
His vasana stands apart and breathes the body.
And when this body cannot satisfy the vasana,
the body is discarded and another body found.
This body is gone; there comes another birth.
The birth is for the fulfillment of that vasana.
Think!
Is it possible to raise both feet at once while walking?
One foot must be down and the other lifted up.
So with the vasana of former birth. *

PART FOUR
SADHANA

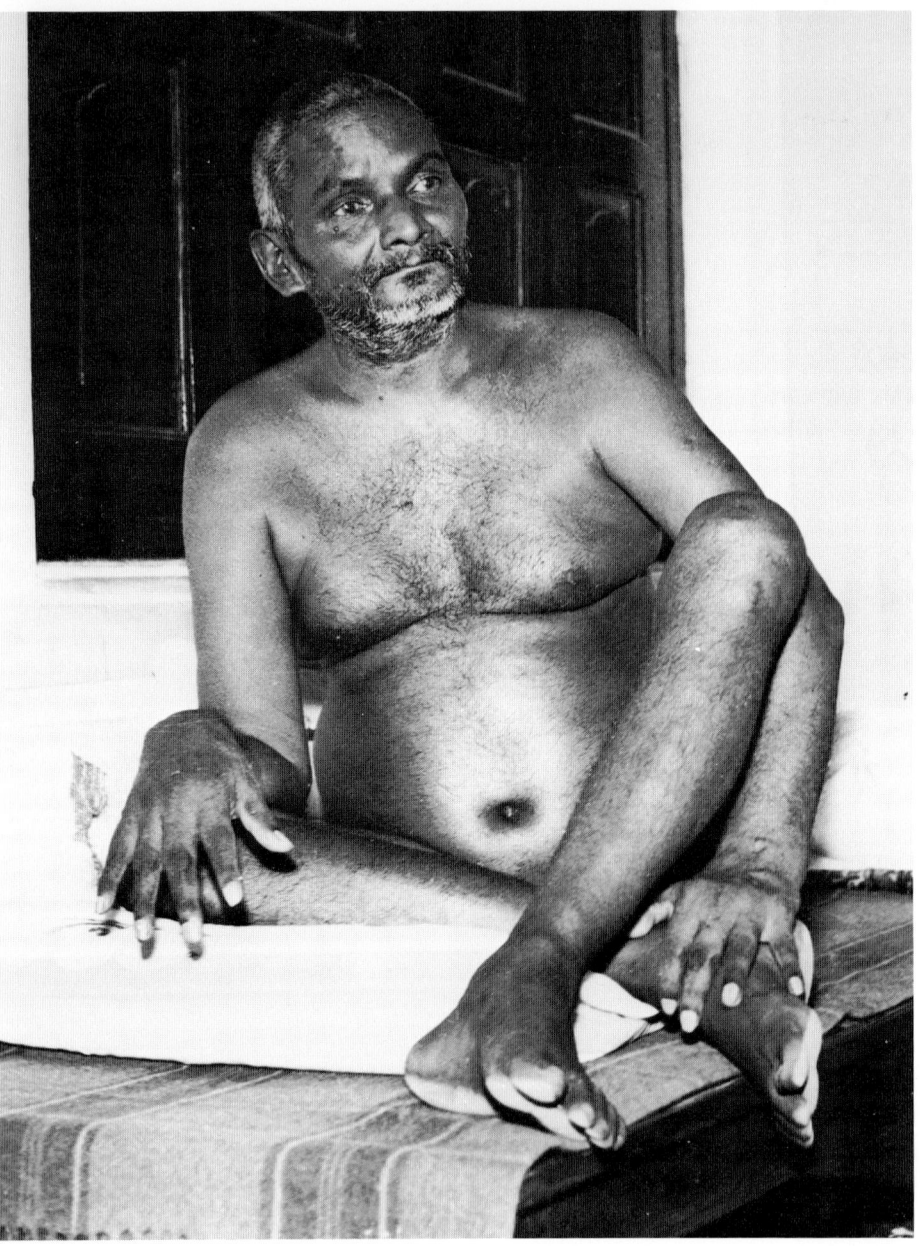

SADHANA

Lakshmansa Khoday was a very great devotee. Just twelve hours before Nityananda's mahasamadhi he arrived at Ganeshpuri and had darshan of the Bhagavan. Seeing the weakened condition of his guru's body, Lakshmansa was moved to tears, and when, even in this condition, the lover of devotees ordered coffee for him, he could bear it no longer. He prayed that Nityananda use his Shakti to cure himself. But Nityananda, the incarnation of love and kindness said: "[The Shakti is] not for this body, [it is] for the bhaktas (devotees)."

As is the custom with many Hindus, the narrator of this incident invited the thin, dark sadhu home to stay for the night, as he was impressed by the bearing of the young man. Given a room, the sadhu asked him for a string. Wondering at this strange request, the host decided to sleep in the same room. When he returned, he was surprised to see the young man carefully attaching the string to swing between two walls. The host was even more surprised a few minutes later, when the young sadhu climbed up on the string, stretched out, and went to sleep! He was apparently totally comfortable, as he turned this way and that, a picture of complete rest and tranquility.

Remembering similar incidents in the life of Sai Baba of Shirdi, the devotee lay there, lost in the sheer wonder of it. In the morning, the young sadhu awoke and, remarking that it was time for the train to Kanhangad to come, went out. Only when the train could be heard leaving the station nearby could the host arise. And only then did he realize that he had been with the great Saint of Kanhangad, Nityananda.

On hearing of Swamiji, fishermen from the coastal area of Kanhangad started flocking to him; their leader's name was Poklon. After he saw devotees bring vegetarian dishes for Nityananda, Poklon brought some cooked rice and curry made of crabs. With great devotion and simplicity, he fed Nityananda the food he had brought; the Bhagavan ate it all and smiled. That night Poklon and his son went out with their fishing nets, only to run into a sudden, savage storm. There was heavy rain, thunder, and high winds; both father and son were knocked unconscious as the boat capsized. They recovered to realize that their boat was righted and they were being towed to shore by an unknown boatman. As their eyes cleared, the men were filled with wonder: the boatman was none other than Nityananda and in their unharmed boat were their nets filled with fish.

A devotee recalls his first chance meeting with Nityananda in Kanhangad. It was 1929; the devotee was traveling with his family to another ashram near Kanhangad, but the railroad porter on hearing of their destination urged them to see Nityananda as well. The porter was very enthusiastic; he said that while Nityananda did not have an official ashram, he was a truly extraordinary saint who was very kind to the poor and lowly no matter what their faith. Interested, they proceeded to the old fort area (where the rock temple was erected in 1963). There was an entrance in the broken wall of the old fort, and the party was told that Nityananda often used this dilapidated gateway.

After a long wait, Nityananda appeared, walking briskly, and entered the old gate. The family hurried after him, but he had disappeared completely, so they returned to the entrance. It was early spring and the mangoes were still ripening on the trees. Some local boys began to throw stones at the tender young fruit when Nityananda reappeared and called to the boys to stop. They immediately changed their target and began hurling stones at the Bhagavan. But before anyone could react, a strange sight met their eyes: each stone that touched Nityananda fell down as a sweet. More stones were thrown and more sweets fell. Without a word, Nityananda walked away and disappeared again into the jungle. The boys were busy collecting sweets. The devotee and his family resumed their journey to the other ashram. They had seen how a saint behaves: giving sweets for stones.

A successful hotelier in Bombay, Kanaran was a loyal devotee, going to Ganeshpuri every Thursday for darshan of Nityananda. In spite of this, he found it impossible to obey when he was ordered to close down his flourishing hotel. (Nityananda's actual words were: "Hotel bandh.") There soon followed calamity after calamity; in an astonishingly short time, Kanaran was reduced to begging for food and shelter from friends. He was deeply ashamed, feeling that his affairs were a shambles and his life a failure. Resolving to put an end to his suffering, he went to the sea shore. He waited until after dusk, when the crowds had cleared. Then, in a final gesture of despair, he threw his useless ring of keys far out into the sea, knowing he himself would soon follow. But before he could move, he heard someone calling his name. Turning, Kanaran recognized a close friend, a man from Gujarat. This friend knew Kanaran's history and knew of his despair; he managed to dissuade him from his plan and took him to a hotel. Incredibly, he produced Kanaran's ring of keys, which should have been deep in the sand of the ocean! Along with the keys, the friend gave the former hotelier some money, then ordered two dinners. Telling the still gaping Kanaran to eat both servings if he did not return soon, the rescuer left. Mysteriously, he did not return and could not be found again.

Times changed and Kanaran again found himself in the long line of devotees waiting for the darshan of Nityananda. When his turn came, Nityananda spoke: "Where is your Gujarati friend?" The smile that accompanied this question revealed the mystery to Kanaran, as he recognized his long-lost "friend." Nityananda then told him how difficult it would have been for him to regain human birth if he had had his way. Reaffirming the necessity of making the best use of the life allotted to him, Kanaran flourished again with Nityananda's blessings.

THE SUTRAS

Without yoga
there is no escape
from the law of karma.

97

98   Only in the subtle can you be without thought.
Discrimination is the merging of mind into buddhi.
Samadhi is the equal vision: seeing One in all.
Through sadhana (spiritual practice), keep the six enemies
—anger, desire, envy, passion, greed, delusion—
under control.
When you practice, do not speak ill of others; if you do,
it is like putting a stone on a young sprouting plant.
Do not relax your practice even for fifteen minutes;
the mind should be ceaselessly kept in the center.

99   Act according to your word,
speak as you intend to act.

Even if you perform *tapas* (purification)   100
for a thousand years
if you work for results
Self-realization will not come.
Perform tapas for even a little while without desire, and
you will see God in all and all in God.

Even a child of five knows there is a God   101
but not where He is.
The sun has been the silent witness of all time
and all events,
Yet how many truly see the sun?
How many people sincerely seek God?
Three-quarters are addicted to the senses,
less than a quarter even reach the middle state.
A few do good deeds, but of evil deeds there are many doers.

102 A true guru can turn you from the jungle road of ignorance
to the royal road of spiritual knowledge.
There are two gurus:
the guru of cause
and the guru of action.
The guru who gives the disciple a mantra (sacred word or formula)
or otherwise initiates him into spiritual practice
is the causal guru.
The Self is the action guru.
No person can be another's action guru,
only another's causal guru.
The causal guru can lead the thirsty disciple to the well,
but it is the inner, action guru that prompts him to drink deeply.
The first instructs, the second acts.
The divine force within all creatures is the Self.
This is the action guru, the supreme guru,
the all-pervading guru,
God.*

People often think the physical teacher is the guru, 103
yet one does not become a guru by wearing orange robes
and wooden sandals or by using prayer-beads.
Preaching about the highest truth but giving the disciples
only stones is not the behavior of a guru.
Only he who lives by his teaching is the true guru.
Before teaching others,
he must complete his own spiritual practices and
attain Self-realization.
Only then can he prove the truth.

To ride a horse safely in a crowd of two thousand people 104
requires a capable rider.
Intelligence is above, mind is below.
Intelligence is king, mind is the minister;
mind must be subordinate to intelligence.
The first is sound, the second is the impression that follows.
The Self is the primary guru,
The secondary guru is the one who initiates.
To do and to teach is the secondary guru,
to realize is the primary.
There is no guru without aspiration.
When you have aspiration, you require the secondary guru.
The secondary guru leads you to the well.
The primary guru drinks from it.

105   He turns darkness into light, ignorance into knowledge.
He reveals the subtle sight in place of the gross.
He is the One guru,
the guru who is in all, the guru of the universe.
No person can be your guru,
a person can only be secondary.
The real guru is Guru of the Universe:
OM, Brahma, Vishnu, the highest, the Absolute, origin of all.
Higher than mental modifications,
higher than the transient maya that adorns the body.
Like the dried coconut separates from the shell,
give up the body-idea.
This is the highest.

106   Fire has spread itself everywhere,
it is the highest of all,
it is essential to all creation.
First realize yourself, then impart it to others;
this is the highest duty.
When you are hungry, realize that others also feel hunger.
When you are in pain, realize that others also feel pain.
What is your goal is also the goal of others.
If a doctor knows a remedy but does not reveal it
before his death, it is lost with him.
He who does not know the way to Self-realization is no man.
Of all ways of knowledge, Self-realization is the highest.
This Self-realization should be made known to all people.
Those who are hungry must be fed.
No one seeks knowledge of the One
without discriminative power.

One who has dissolved the mind is the universal teacher. 107
He has uprooted all desire.
The true renunciate has burned all desire to ashes,
he is the universal teacher.
For those who have renounced desire, the universe is within.
Sannyasa (the spiritual path) is the heart-space,
the akasha,
light, consciousness, divine light, fire,
fire with form, internal fire, fire of discrimination.
The fire of discrimination is in the universe.

Only one who has abandoned all desire 108
is an *acharya* (teacher).
He alone is a sannyasi or an *avadhut*.
The avadhut is the highest of men,
exalted.
There is none higher than this. The avadhut is above all.
To him, this world and the next are one.
He dwells in the sky of consciousness,
the true sky,
the sky of liberation in life (jivanmukti).
Joy, delight, bliss,
ananda, the bliss of self-mastery, of God, of the Real,
of release from all bonds, of human fulfillment.
The avadhut is the lord of liberation,
the king of understanding.

109 The avadhut knows that birth and death
are illusions of the body.
He is no more identified with the body than an ordinary man
is identified with his garments.
He has gone beyond all qualities and
shines with the full glow of Self-realization.
He is at once the light and all that is illuminated,
fully aware,
a raja yogi, not the hatha yogi.
The avadhut has no sense of "I."
He sees all as a projection of Self,
he views all with equal pleasure.
No matter where he wanders, he has no sense of duality.
He is not bothered by thirst or hunger.
If food is available, he eats,
when it is not available, he does not ask for it.
Those who offer him poison or those who offer him milk,
they are the same to the avadhut.
Those who beat him and those who love him,
they are the same to the avadhut.
To the avadhut the universe is father, mother, family.
He contains the entire universe,
the universe is merged in him.

The state of realization means 110
to experience oneness inside.
The microcosm is visible inside, the macrocosm is seen within.
The macrocosm is not created;
creation is a process of the mind, not of the Self.
For the mind, there is fear; for the body, there is creation.
When the world is realized within, there is no fear.
If the body is adorned with gold and jewels,
there is fear.
Those without ornament have no cause for sorrow.
They have the equal vision.
Those who see with the physical eye
see differences, have desires, and are impelled to act.
Desirelessness is liberation;
absence of desire for the fruits of action is jivanmukti:
Self-Realization.
This is the state of the avadhut.
This is the subtle state.
The jnani has the inner sight, he has dissolved the mind,
he experiences the One in all.
He sees no differences—all is One.
Differences belong to the gross state;
the inner breath is not divisible,
it is One.

111   One without a guru does not realize the truth.
In this world there is no effect without a cause.
Spiritual wisdom means seeing light in the world's darkness.
Darkness is ignorance, light is knowledge.
Do not be a hypocrite to earn fame.

112   One whose mind is always at one with the Absolute is a *brahmachari*.
Such a person is on the path to knowledge of God,
even if he is an untouchable.
Wearing orange robes, carrying a *dandi* (walking stick) or
water pot, talking of Vedanta and
arguing about it with everyone,
these things do not make one a swami.

To be fit for the name "guru" 113
one must renounce completely the idea
that "I am the body."
There is none higher than such a guru. God is not higher than
the guru who is identified with the Absolute.
Such a guru is a manifestation of sat-chit-ananda
(the bliss of universal consciousness).
Such a guru is God made manifest.

What you hold in your hand has no scent, no value; 114
what you receive from others has scent and value.
The highest yoga is eternal bliss,
the all-pervading OM, pranava,
the universal teacher is eternal bliss.

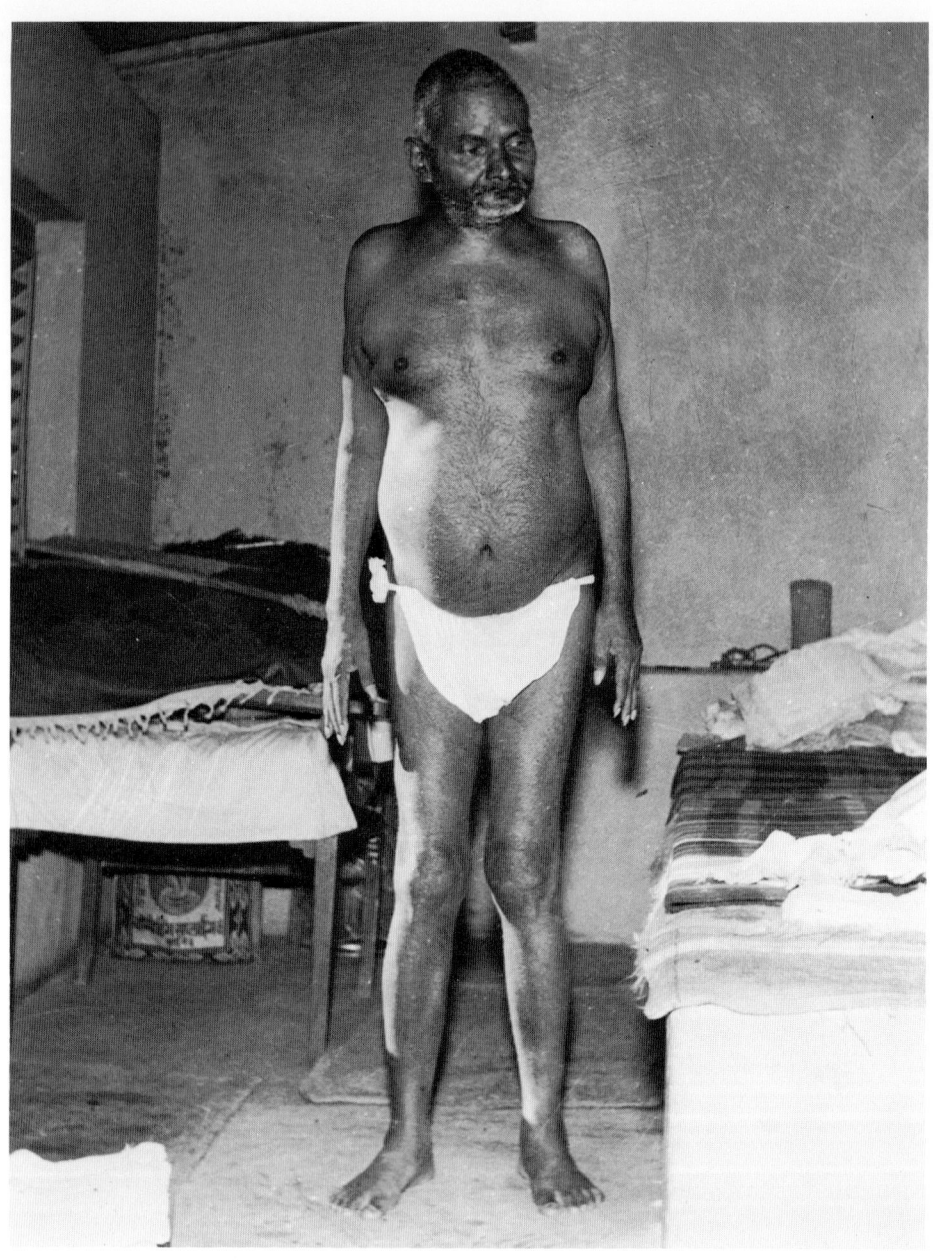

Nityananda in Kailas. Many photos show him sitting on the concrete platform to the right.

Devotion is *prema* (intense, divine love). 115
Giving food and drink is not devotion, not love.
This is a delusion of the mind, it pertains only to the body.
Learn to eat and drink the subtle food;
drink the waters of discrimination.
Peace is water; to settle in the water of peace is
the joy of yoga.
O mind!
Leave worldly pleasures and turn to eternal delight,
leave worldly joy and enjoy eternal joy.
Enter into the eternal,
run into the heart.
The divine is in the heart, the real joy is in the heart,
your own liberation is in the heart.
Live in this joy.
Enter the internal, leave the external.
Open the third eye and see the world with "same-sightedness."

If you look at ten people, 116
their devotion will not be identical in nature.
If ten people are traveling on foot together and
one person sits down to rest,
the other nine will soon sit.
Likewise, devotion begins with one person.
Seeing it, hearing it,
devotion arises in others.

117   Everyone does not get hungry at the same time,
everyone does not reach liberation at the same time.
There are differences in timing.
Men quarrel and debate because of differences in language:
one says "mittha," another "sakkare," but it is all sugar,
it is the same for all.
No matter how it is used, it goes to the same place.
Instead of believing in thousands of gods,
believe in only one God and find happiness, contentment.
Those who believe in thousands of gods are never content.
As long as there are two, there is no happiness.
Find happiness in one. God is only one, never two.
When this is your faith, you see God in yourself,
you see all as Self.
This is the path to *moksha*: liberation.
Then there is no enemy, all are friends.
Do not court harm by believing in two,
believe in one and reach liberation.
Return to your origin.
Know cause and effect; play on the stage,
then return to your origin and find liberation.
Liberation does not come to search for you,
you must seek liberation, you must make the effort.
What is this liberation?
It is detachment from actions,
detachment from the internal state.
It is not attained by any outward path,
it is not different from your Self.
You have not really worked to reach liberation,
that is why it looks so far away to you.
Liberation is not reached by running here or going there;
search inside yourself.
Merge the mind in buddhi,
follow the path of discrimination to liberation.
God is infinite.

Man makes images and calls them God.
This is ignorance.
Shake it off and follow the path of discrimination to liberation
in this life.
The love you have for an object is a kind of devotion.
Trust whatever you have followed with faith that gave results;
this belief should not lessen.
There is nothing without devotion.
All creatures have devotion.
Like water, devotion can flow in many ways,
all creatures have a right to devotion.
It is there, full, in all.
Pure devotion, bhakti, is attained through the heart-sky.
Turning inward, bhakti shall know the subtle.
There, one is desireless, without care:
this is eternal liberation.
Reach it through the path of the sushumna.

As is your devotion, so is your liberation.   118
Good work brings good wages,
a little work brings only a little wage.

119　　If water is added to a cup that is already full,
it overflows.
When a person is filled with perfect peace,
it becomes known to all.
Such a person has no desires.
this is the highest peace, full peace,
Union.

120　　Desireless devotion does not promise
enjoyment in the world.
Devotion is not related to nature,
it is not intended to eliminate difficulties.
There is no relation whatsoever
between devotion and difficulty.
It is not of the body.
True bhakti never turns back, it always moves forward.
Embrace the heart firmly with devotion,
hold tight with steadfast faith,
whatever the difficulty.
By the path of skill (yukti) bhakti is united with Shakti.

Such a heart is purified of desire,
joined to pure renunciation.
Let the desirelessness strengthen, let the senses be quieted.
OM is All: the creator of the universe, the granter of peace.
Let your devotion be steady in this creator, this giver of peace;
this is the best devotion.
This is eternal peace, Self-luminous, the essence of being (sat).
Such devotion is beyond this world and beyond the next;
it is nothing but the mind filled with eternal delight.
The mind filled with eternal delight
is the seed of all things.
Nourish the seed with discrimination.
The mind filled with eternal delight is without qualities,
without disease, without blemish, without sin.
It is the universal reason,
the Creator,
the Witness of All,
the universal Being,
the One in all,
all knowledge,
the one cause and effect,
the universal Witness, universal Guru,
universal Father and Mother,
the OM Bindu,
OM of "me - a - i"
the Supreme, the Moveable, the Seen, OM the Essence:
OM OM OM

121 Giving food or money to charity is not devotion.
Universal love is devotion.
Seeing God in all beings is devotion.
Looking with equal-sightedness is devotion.

122 When you walk in the dark, there is fear,
but not so in daylight.
Darkness is ignorance, light is knowledge.
The guru is light, light is the guru.

Fear is an imagination of the mind. 123
To the inner eye, there is no fear.
It is impossible for the blind man to describe a cart.
For the man without a guru, there is no place in the world.

Everything comes from inside, not from outside. 124
You become evil by yourself, you become good by yourself.
The breath of Omkar should be inside you,
then there is purity.
When evil is merged in good, it is transformed into good.

125   If you are afraid of water, you cannot cross the river
even in a boat.
If you are afraid of fire, you cannot even cook a meal.
There must be no fear.
For anything to be done,
first you must have courage.

126   A good man sees everyone as good.
A person becomes good by his own effort.

Remain in the center of the glance of the guru. 127
The mind must be kept steady and firm,
not flickering like the reflection of sun in moving water.

In the beginning devotion may be selfish, 128
but in time, all desires turn toward the Self.
The whole world becomes the guru.

129   The *asana* (yoga posture) is the station;
a good posture is raja yoga.
Asana is posture.

130   At birth a child is perfect and free,
at death also there is perfection and freedom.
In between, there is delusion.
That which pervades in all four directions is the One,
indivisible;
within it is the many,
divisible.

When a child is born of the womb, there are differences   131
based on time.
The nature of the child is affected
by the thought of the parents,
whether it be devotion, deceit, anger, activity, desire.
Life begins when vayu enters the womb.
If the parents think of this world or of the next world,
the child will have the same inclination.
If the thought is of the next world,
sudden enlightenment is possible.

Young children do not think about their parents,   132
only as they grow do they begin to know the mother and the father.
When a chicken eats, it scratches every particle towards its feet.
As the mind develops, selfishness grows.
Every day people are born, every day people die,
but rarely is selfishness given up.
But it is possible to give it up completely.
When the identity is merged with the indivisible universal Self,
all selfishness burns up.
Many kinds of food are prepared from rice,
such as halva and ambada;
these dishes are not called rice.

133   A ripe banana is sweet, the green fruit is hard and sour.
Yet both fruits grow on the same tree,
only time is different.
When you plant a coconut in the ground,
it does not produce fruit immediately,
it does not even produce the tree immediately.
First the tender shoot appears, then the young sapling,
after years, the tree, and only then, the fruit.
The young plant is easily uprooted, the old tree stands firm.
So also the mind should stand firm,
whatever people say to you or about you.
This is what you must accomplish in this life,
this should be your sole purpose.
Persist towards this goal at all costs,
even when your head may be chopped off.
Learn to bind up without rope;
this is man's purpose in this life.

The sun is reflected both in the salty waves of the sea   134
and in the clear surface of a mountain lake.
Seeing things with the physical eyes is not enough.
You must experience the inner significance of the thing seen.

Give up honor and pride, give up love of body.   135
Only then can you see God everywhere
and in every being.

136   Vairagya (renunciation) born upon seeing dead bodies
burning at the cremation ground
is temporary.
This is also the truth of the body: it is temporary.
Desirelessness given by the guru
should be held and cultivated;
such renunciation leads to liberation.
This vairagya is first,
the guru is second,
desire for guidance and initiation is third.
You must practice renunciation yourself.
Experience true desirelessness;
this is the highest attainment of human life.
To achieve vairagya and to impart it to others
is the highest attainment of yoga.
It is indivisible, it is the Tree of Peace.
Climb the tree of peace within the head,
at the top is the imperishable desirelessness.
The first vairagya is to renounce desire and anger.
The second vairagya is to live in the world,
taste its pleasures,
and then renounce them.
True desirelessness is the state of the jivanmukti:
liberation in this life.

Money, jewels, status, authority, power: 137
these cause fear and striving.
Fear of losing them and
striving for more.
Fear of death,
for death will bring an end to the sense-pleasures.
Without these, there is no fear.

At the moment of death, it is Shiva that saves you, 138
not Hari (Lord of the Outer Nature).
In Shiva there is Shakti,
in Hari there is maya.
The body is of the earth, bodily senses all look outward.
Shiva is internal, He is the Brahmarandhra.
This knowledge cannot be taught by another.
This knowledge must be experienced.

139   It is rare to be a millionaire,
all cannot be millionaires at the same time.
Everyone is rewarded according to his due.
There is plenty of water in the sea;
how much water you get depends
on the size of the container you bring.
The residue of past actions determines the fruit.
It is because of these past actions
that you are interested in the teachings of holy men.
It is because of these past actions
that you find no pleasure in the world.
For those who are so guided,
there is no need for special renunciations,
vairagya itself is the result of past actions.
For such people, now is the time to pursue liberation.

140   Now—before you die—leave the jungle road
and follow the royal road.
On your death bed you may suffer
if the prana is obstructed by disease.
Purify the breath and consciousness now.

Vairagya is like fire burning cloth: 141
the greater the vairagya, the greater the splendor from within.
The mind, not the body, should be firmly seated.
If your mind is not pure,
how can you develop equal-sightedness?
If you do not practice, how can you develop balance?
Through practice, the subtle intelligence develops,
and the desire for objects disappears.
It is difficult to give up attachment
to possessions, women, gold. What is the purpose of life?
Merge the mind and the properties into One,
become one-pointed.
Dirty linen is renewed by washing in soap and water.
Purify the mind in the water of buddhi and
it will be as pure as akasha.
When you first use a treadle sewing machine,
your attention is not on the legs but on the hands.
Carefully place the buddhi,
merge mind and thought in the heart-space, and attain peace.
This is nityananda; eternal bliss.*

True worship is not performed by the hands 142
or by the mouth.
The Self is not realized by the mind.
Action, work, is not performed by the hands
nor by the legs.
O mind! Act with no desire for results,
do work without attachment.
Attain desirelessness and see all equally.

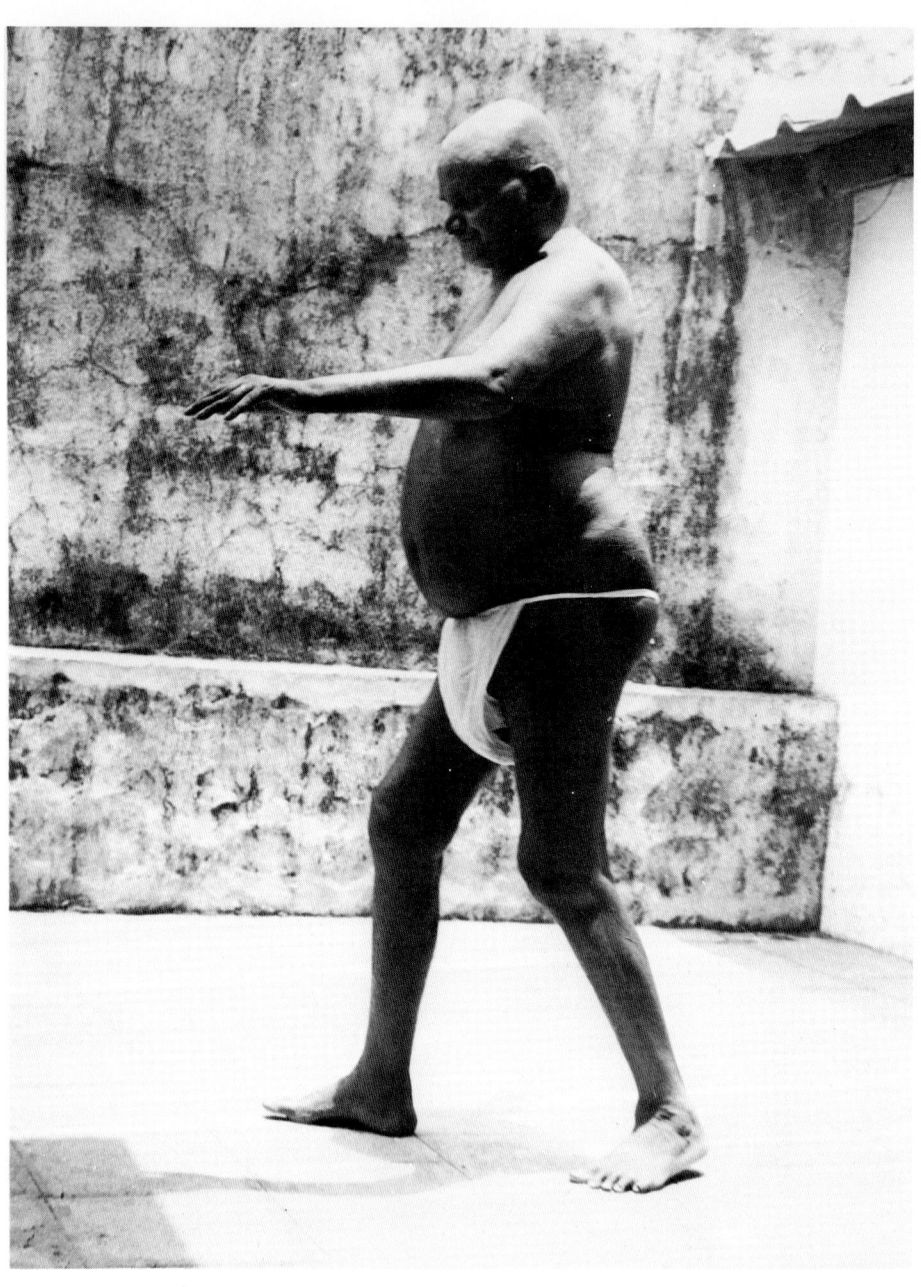
Courtyard, Kailas. In his last years, Nityananda seldom left the Kailas compound in Ganeshpuri.

From one coconut come thousands of coconuts. 143
But if the trunk of the coconut tree is cut,
the fruits cease.
Attachment is like the trunk.
Sever it with the axe of discrimination,
then comes peace.
The properties of harmony, balance and inner peace
all come from non-attachment.
A steady intellect (buddhi) yields sattva-guna,
perfect balance.
Truth is like letters engraved in stone,
the talk of ordinary men is like letters written in chalk.

On a single mango tree, 144
not all fruits grow and ripen at the same time.
First there is the tender young fruit,
in its own time it ripens.
The ripe fruit is good to eat.
Be like the mango fruit.
Be at peace in everything.

145 He is a brahmin who has experienced
the joy of the Absolute.
Maya is transient.
O Hari, burn the ego!
One who has destroyed mind has destroyed delusion.
Maya is not the Lord, Shiva is the Lord.
Everyone knows there is butter in milk; when milk has been
boiled, butter can be churned out.
But so few take the butter.
Milk is bhakti, love and devotion.
Heating the milk on fire is the power of discrimination,
the vessel for discrimination is the intelligence, buddhi.
The fire is the fire of yoga.
In this fire, the six enemies of the body
—anger, desire, envy, passion, greed, delusion—
are destroyed and the butter extracted.

146 When gold is melted in fire, its dross is burned away and
it glows with lustrous purity. To purify yourself,
desire, passion, and anger
must be destroyed within.
All activity takes place within,
all exertion is directed within.
The mind does not remain in one state.

An object buried in filth has no value.   147
But if it is removed and cleaned, everyone may use it.
If you find a diamond in the mire, you do not throw it away.

When a ripe coconut is freshly picked and opened,   148
the kernel inside is closely bound to the inside of the shell.
Any damage to the outer shell also damages the kernel.
But when the coconut is left on the tree
or exposed to the sun, the water inside evaporates and
the dried kernel separates from the shell,
making a noise when shaken.
Similarly one must realize that the inner Self
is distinct from the body.
The fire of this knowledge burns up all shortcomings,
like the water in the coconut is burned away by the sun.
The mind then shines like purified gold.

149   Just as the deep glow of pure gold is revealed
after repeated heating,
so the inner is made luminous through the
heat of concentration.
Let the world be illuminated within.
This is one means: the Way of Buddhi.
Perfect one-pointedness, dharana, is understanding;
it approaches the Thought of the Atman.
Experience does not come from words,
words flow from experience.
The tree is in the seed, the seed is not in the tree.
Man is not in the world, the world is in man,
the world is subject to man.
Speak the words your mind thinks,
let there be no deceit or malice in your heart.
Deceive no one. Hate no one.
In the company of others, live always within;
keep the mind one-pointed.
The deceitful heart is like the face of the sun
during monsoon.
At times, a star breaks through the clouds
and shines with glory, but in minutes it is hidden again.
Man's nature changes within five minutes.
The ego-mind falls into the Self like a shooting star
falls from the sky.
The sky of the heart is not visible to the physical eye,
only to the subtle eye.
Through thinking, know the Thought;
through sound, know the Sound;
through mind, know the Mind.

Low activities and a mean disposition indicate   150
a lack of good sense.
It is this lack of sense that marks the pariah,
the untouchable,
the outcast.
Laughing and mocking others, lying, pride, jealousy,
these are the characteristics of the outcast.
It is not black skin or black clothes that make an outcast.
Nor do a turban or a wristwatch or a suit
indicate an admirable man.
Neither are poverty and hunger the signs of an outcast.
No.
He is an outcast who is selfish,
who sees nothing but differences.
If he does not realize the truth of Vedanta, he is no man.
Careful study of Vedanta, like a well-trained horse,
leads to liberation in this life.
But study that is like the wild elephant is not freedom,
only delusion.

Even the worst "sinner"   151
can be changed into a Knower of Truth
in an instant.
There is no sunlight when there are clouds.
The instant the clouds scatter, the sun is visible.
OM is the City of Peace,
the form of Peace.
Give respect and gratitude to OM.

152   Board the train for Kashi.
Travel to "Shivanandapuri," the city of the bliss of Shiva,
in the country of *Shanti* (peace).
The journey ends at "Brahmanandapuri,"
the city of the bliss of God.*

153   Look to God who resides in the heart-space;
yes, you must see God in your heart.
To see God with the inner eye is
the experience of eternal bliss.
It is delusion to mistake a stone image for God.
All pain, all sorrow are delusion.
Praise God within,
praise God in your heart,
praise God in your head.
Discover the secret of the Self that is eternal delight;
yes, you must know that secret.
Look into your heart with the inner eye and
discover the royal road.
Leave the downward path and take to the middle path.
To adorn the external body without knowing the inner secret,
this is the downward path.

Nobody wants a tree without fruit. 154
Why is man called man?
Because he has *manas*: the reflective power of mind.
Use your mind to get knowledge and then unite with peace,
finally become one with Omkar.
Liberation, eternal life, is only possible
when you give up the idea that "I am the body,"
only then can you realize the Self.
It is very difficult for those who think "I am the body"
to see the Self.
Those who cling to the body-idea cannot gain
even the smallest bit of peace,
even if they perform sadhana for a thousand years.
Anyone can bathe in a river and cleanse the body;
whether one is a brahmin or a pariah or a child,
whoever bathes will be cleansed.
The spirit in all is also the same,
only the exterior forms differ.
Chillies and watermelons can grow in the same field,
even though their natures are different.
Only those who sit near the fire will feel its warmth,
not those who sit in water.
Peace is cool, like water. One's nature is like fire.
Food must be prepared before you are hungry.
Know the duties of a householder
before you become a householder.
The householder should be equally attracted
to the inner and the outer.
He should distinguish clearly between cause and effect.

155   It is futile for man to run after the horse;
let him ride it instead.
Bind the horse's feet and mount quickly.
It is also futile to chase the pleasures of the world.
Keep your mind free of attachments.
As water slips off an umbrella, so the idea that
"I am the doer" should pass from you.
The householder must be like the calf dedicated to the temple;
all should be offered to God.
Yet you cannot say that the one who does this is close to God,
and the one who does not do it is far from Him.
If you put a light before a thousand people,
it shines on them all, without distinction.
Anyone may take it.
Where there is light, there is no darkness,
in darkness there is no light; either one or the other.
Your nature should be like the sun,
the mind should be as cool as the moon.

156   Fire, water, earth, and air are available to and used
by everyone.
Water coming through a pipe can be used equally
by the brahmin, the untouchable, or the child,
with no distinction.*

It is not that "this one" has more and another has less. 157
The faculties of thinking, the ear,
the nose,
the hands,
the eyes
are the same for all.*

When a tree is hewn into planks 158
the saw moves up and down,
so it must be with the breath.
It should be induced in the buddhi and moved always upward.
It takes great effort to roll a huge rock
to the top of a hill,
it can roll down without difficulty.
Just so it is difficult to ascend and easy to descend.
It is difficult for the prana to leave the cage of the body.
To receive something is easy,
to return what has been given is difficult.
Nevertheless, they who do not return what has been given are
less than men, they are animals,
without virtue.

159 Find out who you are, look deeply and find out.
"Other" is not the truth, cultivate the "same."
Reach deeply within for the secret;
the sense of separateness is not the truth.
Your words and actions should show "sameness."
Burn the physical sight
and look.
It is the sense of separateness
that causes suffering at the time of death.

160 With faith,
stabilize the breath of life in an upward direction.
This is the path to liberation.
The eternal spirit (jiva) dwells in the cave of the body.
Yoga is union.
When the two merge into one, that is yoga.
When the mind and the buddhi become one, that is yoga.
When the jiva follows the path of buddhi and
enters the Brahmarandhra, that is yoga.
Devotion, reflection, power, all three merge and become OM.
The ego melts into the OM-sound like camphor melts in fire.
The mental processes merge in the Self.
Place the mind in buddhi,
like a child placed in the cradle and rocked.
Know who you are.

The OM-sound should be drawn inside with the breath   161
like water is drawn up from a well.
And like the pot is let down into the well for a fresh fill,
so the exhalation should be released with OM.

Without concentration on the breath, there is no aim,   162
no state, no intelligence, and no fulfillment.
Concentrate.
Think without losing concentration.
Concentrate on the inbreath and the outbreath.
Draw the breath evenly, properly.
Concentrate on the sound of the breath,
breathe and concentrate on the internal sound.
Have faith in that sound, and breathe in.
Breathe deeply and more deeply.
Breathe so the internal sound is audible to the ears.
Do not think of anything else.
Eating, drinking, walking, standing
do not elevate the soul.
Do your own work,
do not desire to eat what others have cooked.
With faith, do what you have to do.

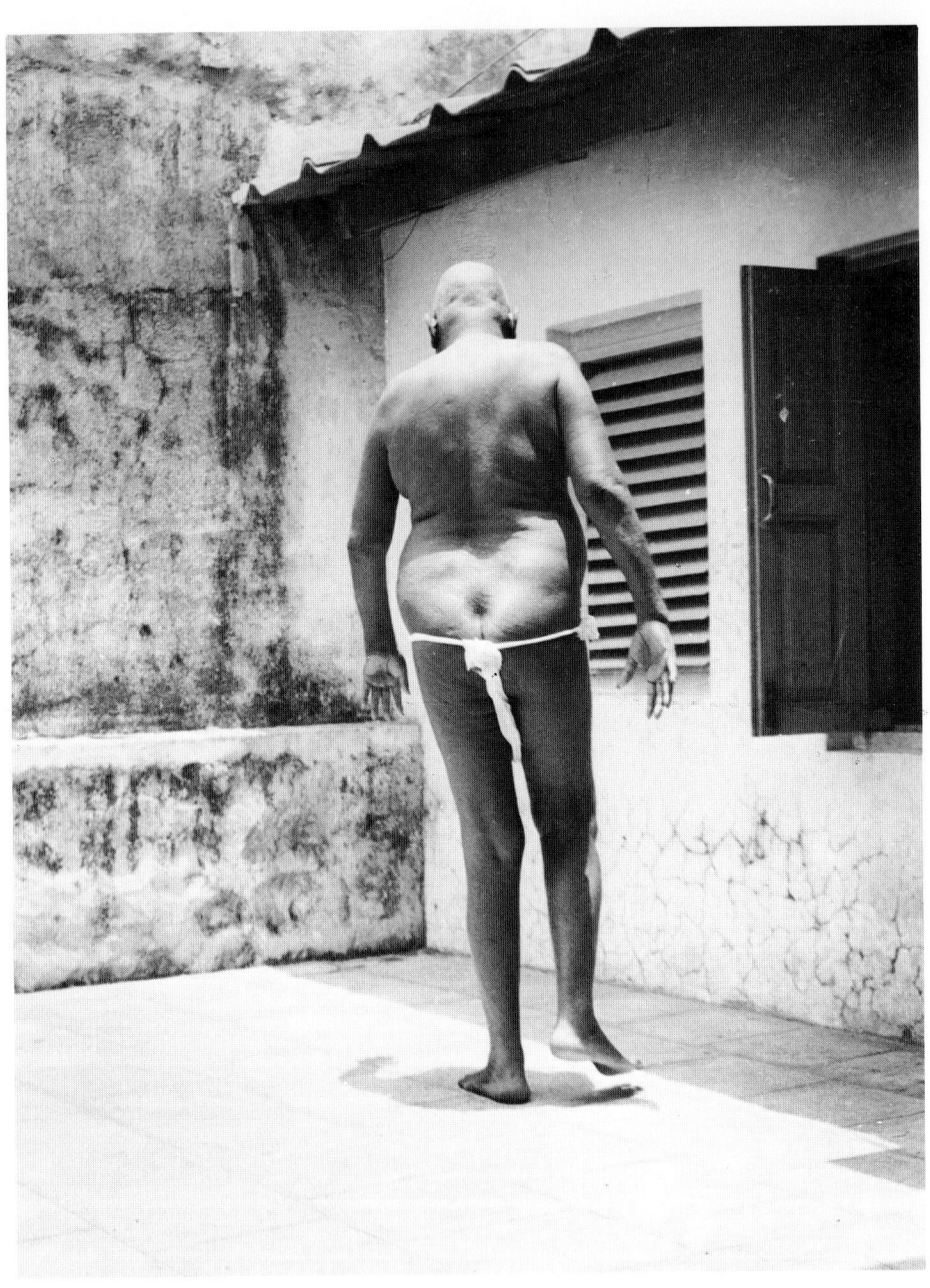

Courtyard, Kailas, Ganeshpuri, c. 1960.

The heart of Vedanta is prana, 163
bringing the breath under complete control.
Vedanta is the knowledge of the Indivisible.
The Veda mantras are not to be uttered by the tongue,
but from the throat.
One who knows this secret is a brahmin.
The sound of OM itself constitutes the Vedas.
It is the light of divine wisdom, the fire of intuition.
Vedanta has no form, it is indivisible, changeless.
It is identical to the Self.
Right utterance of Veda is perfect concentration of the mind.*

If the breath is not harmonious and rhythmical, 164
the fire within is reduced to a dull glow.
Without fire, food is not digested properly.
The free flow of air and energy is obstructed:
water cannot flow through a blocked pipe.
This imbalance leads to all disease.

165   Without control of the breath,
one cannot be a sannyasi or a yogi.
A boat without a rudder cannot be steered.

166   You must allow the breath to move upward freely.
It requires great effort to move a stone uphill,
but it comes down suddenly, without effort.
Concentration is the same.
It is easy to take birth, it is difficult to leave this body.
Discover the source of the river,
it is no use seeking it after it has joined the sea.
To a tree, its central root is most important,
all others are secondary.
Lift a chair and your breath moves upward;
that is the seat of prana.
When cooking, both the flame and the smoke move upward.
In the chimney, the movement is upward.
In the heart-space, the movement of breath is also upward.
Joy is caused by this motion.
Without this motion, there is no circulation of blood.
When a river is dammed, the motion of water is stopped.
In the body such a dam is made of the three humors:
wind, phlegm, and bile.

In pranayama there are three kinds of breath: 167
inhalation, retention, and exhalation.
These processes are internal, nothing is taken from outside.
When, with practice, the breath is controlled,
it becomes centered in the sushumna nadi.
In this state, joy and bliss flow within.
O Brahmananda!
You forget the world, you forget the body;
there is only the world beyond, only *Brahma-loka,* only God.

The best of cobras have the internal breath, 168
they listen attentively to the sweet music of the flute.
The jnani loves all people, all things,
as thoroughly as the cow loves her calf.
This is "same-sightedness."
There can be no house without doors,
no cooking without utensils.
The dog will eat
whether the food is on a golden dish or a stone dish.
The bird thinks only of today's needs, not tomorrow's.
A seed kept in a box will never grow,
it cannot yield fruit.
But this same seed, if placed in soil, will sprout
and yield fruit.
You must practice, you must experience.
You yourself are responsible for either
happiness or misery.

169	There is no house without doors,
no hot water without fire, no fire without air,
no life without food.
Without the life-breath one cannot live
even for a few seconds.

170	Do not be satisfied with scraps left on plates at a feast.
Insist on a fresh serving of food.
Only by *doing* can you enjoy the bliss that flows from the
experience of the divine.

Those who do not breathe through the mouth or nostrils   171
have no desires.
Their breath is purely internal.
They draw the breath up to the Brahmarandhra
where the ida and pingala meet.
They realize themselves as the Self,
they look upon all things as Self.
This is *swarajya* (self-government).
This is the true goal of human life.
The light of life is the prana-vayu, the vital air,
freedom is the capital.
The Lord of the swarajya government is the Self.
Swarajya is one's own Shakti,
it must be kept in one's possession.
Complete freedom is not a hill, it is not gold.
Keeping both desire and anger under perfect control
brings complete freedom.
Both speech and action must be the same.*

Suffering given by God is no suffering,   172
grief given by God is no grief.
It is a delusion of the mind.
There is grief at birth
and grief at the end;
man comes from his mother's womb with tears in his eyes.*

173   Human beings are the highest of all creatures.
There is no incarnation higher than man.
Those who think deeply and fix firmly on the Self
are the very highest.

174   If an evil person falls in the well,
what should be done?
Pull him up.
Do not think that the bad will always be bad,
lead them to the right road.

In the beginning, before perfect peace is attained,
the play of maya is greatly increased.
Wherever you turn, there is the serpent.
In the beginning, when you sit to practice, you may feel
as heavy as a mountain,
as if you are leaving the ground,
as if you are sitting in the sea,
as if hot water were being poured on you,
as if you were sitting high above and observing,
as fine and subtle as the point of a needle,
as insubstantial as a leaf.
You may not be able to say
whether you are walking, talking, or sitting.
At times, all feelings cease,
you are as still and rooted as the coconut tree.
You may look about and see
only actors in a dramatic performance.
You may see black faces.
In perfect peace, all is infinite white light.
Light in darkness, darkness in light.
The universe is in darkness, in the universe is light.
At times, everything looks like a movie on a screen,
at other times, only sat-chit-ananda is seen.
Questions arise:
"Why have I come into this world?"
"Where am I going?"
"What is my duty?"
Coming down is not permanent,
but going up
step by step
to the upper story is permanent.
All that is seen, all that is heard, all that is done
is like a net that cannot be cut through.
All-penetrating OM is the all-penetrating pranava.

175

176 The ear would be of no use in place of the eye.
The work given to the legs should be done by the legs;
the hands are not suited for walking.
The hands do their work
but they cannot think;
thinking is done by the brain.
Each person must do that for which he is suited.

177 Your hunger is not satisfied by the smell of food,
you must eat the food to be satisfied.
Experience is necessary; when you have experienced truth,
no one can oppose you.
You cannot experience the sweetness of sugar
if you hold it in your hand, you must put it in your mouth.
This is experience.
Knowledge gained from books leaves room for
doubt and questioning.
Experience is certain.

The actor first rehearses his role in privacy,   178
then he performs for others.
Conduct your initial practices in secret,
later this is not necessary.

Cow's milk never tastes bitter,   179
a statue does not speak.
Merely visiting holy places like Kashi and Rameshwar
does not bring liberation.
First silence the mind and establish it in the Self,
then concentrate deeply, with spiritual discernment.
Stone or clay statues and ritualistic worship
do not reveal God.
If the true significance of the statue or of the ceremony
is not comprehended,
liberation is not possible.
Human birth is the effect, giving it back is the cause.
Comprehending properly, removing the primordial ignorance,
and dedicating this life to seeking the true source,
this leads to the the peace of liberation.

180   Holding sugar in the palm of the hand does not lead to knowledge of its sweetness.
Only by eating sugar can its sweetness be known.
Mere repetition of holy names like Rama, Krishna, and Govinda, even for a thousand years,
cannot bring liberation.
Mantra must be repeated with full knowledge, devotion, and concentration.

181   Abstain from gross sleep, sleep in the subtle state.
Rest in concentration on the internal breath.

In the beginning of practice, sleep less. 182
When eating sparingly, do not bathe in cold water;
frequent cold water baths affect blood circulation.

For liberation and wisdom, age is no consideration. 183
This is the moment.
If you are hungry, you should eat.
If you are not hungry, you should wait.
The hunger for devotion must be intense.
The larger the fire, the sooner the water boils.
Intense faith is the heat, peace is like ice in the head,
it fills the inside and overflows to the outside.
Fully satisfied, the mind becomes pure.
This peace, this contentment, costs nothing,
not even a penny like charity.
When one is filled with this peace,
those around him also benefit.
When it begins in one, it begins in others also.
Even among thousands, if one has this peace,
others also enjoy a part of it.
When entering a crowd of people,
a holy man should have the peace of the hunter
approaching a tiger.
To live in the world, a holy man must have great calm,
great peace.
Peace is of great help in moving among thousands of people.

184   Fire consumes anything and everything,
it makes no distinction between good or evil.
Those who work also can consume anything.
Those who do not work
don't know what must be done.
They get indigestion.
One whose fire is active can eat anything,
it will be digested.
Sleep also in moderation.
Do not eat to a full stomach.
In all things be regular.

185   There is no strict rule about food or diet.
Eat satisfying food, but in moderation.
Eating should be moderate and regular.
This is the only rule.
Fill half the stomach with food, a quarter with water,
leave a quarter unfilled.
Do not indulge in too much sleep.

Many different things are brought to a fair. 186
Peace can be pursued in many ways.
Amid thousands, remain steadfast.
As an airplane moves without the help of the earth,
so you must move without concern for the body.
Plant the conviction "I am not the body" firmly in your heart.
Just as a traveler, weary from walking under the hot sun,
forgets his fatigue as soon as he rests on a shaded hillside,
so a person who rests in the knowledge of the supreme
forgets his worldly troubles.
As soon as you enter the cool, you forget the heat,
so the idea of "I" and "mine" is forgotten.
No umbrella is needed inside the house,
it is only needed outside.
When you sit inside the house and lock all the doors,
you see nothing but the inside of the house.
It is only when you open the doors that the outside is seen.
Learn to open and shut the doors of the senses.
When the warehouse is locked, all business stops.
When the senses are shut,
there is no difference between inside and outside.
Take care with the senses,
they are like a horse that must be reined.
Keep your attention fixed on the senses,
as fixed as a nail in the wall.
Keep the attention above the neck, never below the neck.

187   From a distance
the train and the rails appear to be joined together
but really they are separate.
The rails are pre-set by gross nature,
the train is moved by the steam of subtle discrimination.
The connection between body and spirit must be examined
by the subtle intelligence, then peace is attained.
As the railroad cars are connected into one train,
so let the individual and the Self be connected.
Sever the bonds of the physical qualities;
let the jiva reach eternal liberation.

188   If water is heated in a tightly closed vessel,
all the heat energy is held in.
Water flows from the pump making the OM-sound.
Abandon the wild jungle path and take the royal road,
take the downward-moving energy and move it upward.
The mind should know its place.

Changing the outward appearance 189
without realizing the truth within
does not change the karma.
One does not become a renunciate by
putting on the clothing and mannerisms of a monk
while keeping deceit within.
Parasite!
Hypocrite!
Speak what is in your mind, act as you speak.
One who has attained unity of body, mind, and speech,
whose actions fit his words
and whose words are true to the inner Self,
that one is the real sannyasi, yogi, *paramahamsa*, jnani.
The sannyasi gives up desire.
One who gives up desire is the guru.*

Sat is the indivisible, subtle thought; 190
Chit is always changing.
When sat is merged with chit, the result is ananda:
bliss, joy, delight.
This is satchitananda, nityananda, *paramananda*.
When jivatman joins paramatman, the result is ananda:
yogananda, paramananda, satchitananda, Brahmananda,
Nityananda.

COMMENTARY

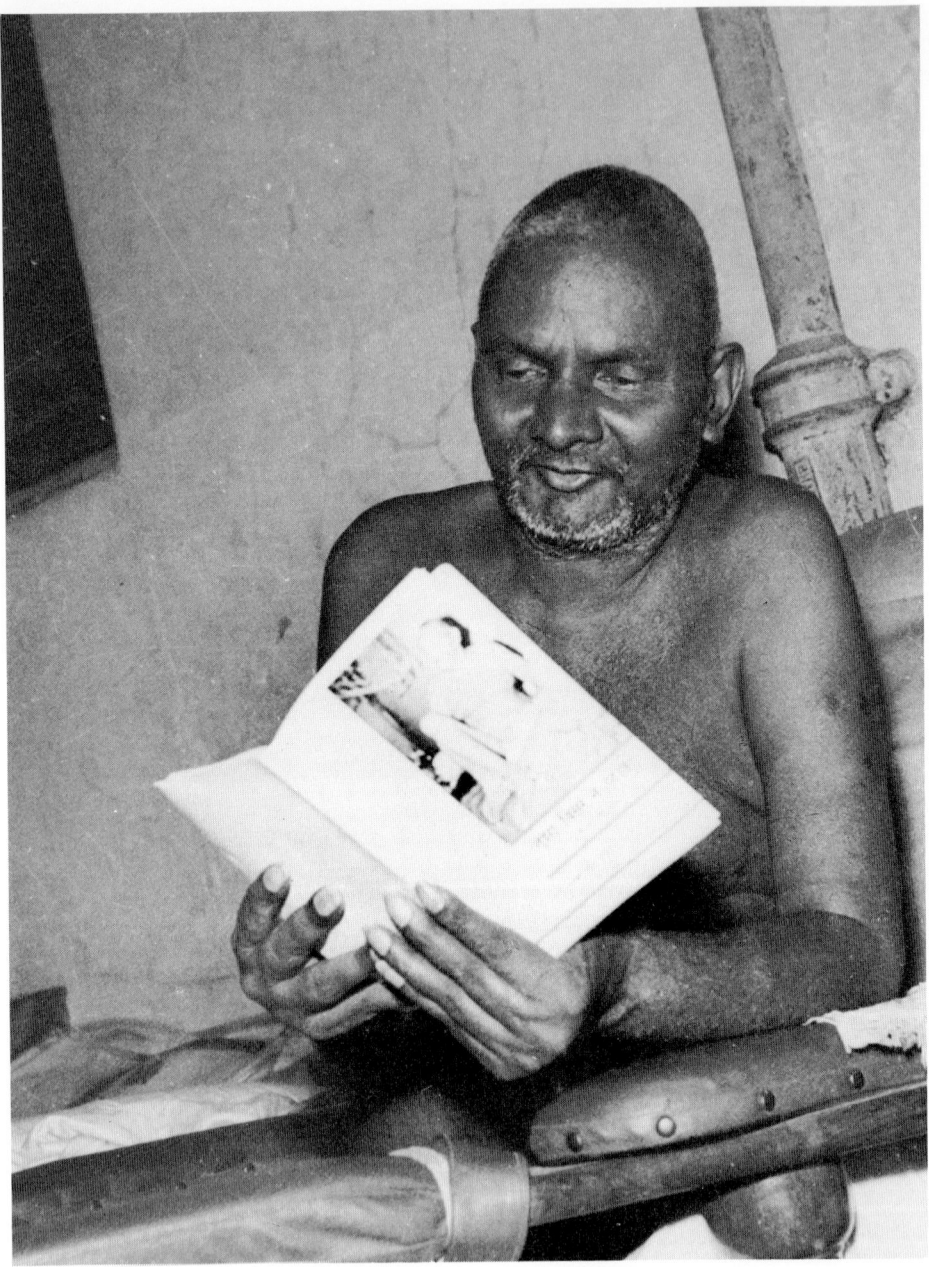

COMMENTARY

Sutra 1 *Atman* is used interchangeably with *Self* in these sutras. Atman refers to the universal Self that manifests as a proliferation of rays emanating from itself. These rays are not different from the nature of their source, but only take on the appearance of separateness. *Kundalini* is the Supreme conscious energy manifesting as an individuated person (*jivatman*). *Paramatman* is the Absolute. Both are Atman. It is the merging of Atman into Atman, like the merging of waves into water, that is the goal of spiritual practice: the union of the individual and the Divine. The Absolute, the Supreme, Paramatman, Brahman, the Self are all synonymous with Atman in these sutras.

The image of *chidakash* is also central to Nityananda's teaching as given in these sutras; the word is formed of the roots *chit*, consciousness, and *akasha*, space or sky, and is thus poetically translated as the sky of consciousness. It is synonymous with *hridayakasha*, sky of the heart. When the original Kanarese edition of Nityananda's words was prepared for printing, his devotees asked him to suggest a title. He replied simply that the words had come from chidakash, and thus the work was entitled *Chidakash Gita*.

As discussed in the Introduction, chidakash is an experience; it is a state of consciousness in which perception is objectless and limitlessly vast, a state in which the individual and the universal are in complete union. In various disciplines, this experience of Oneness may be called *samadhi, turiya, nirvana,* or *shunya*. Surface distinctions notwithstanding, there is no essential difference among these terms.

Nityananda also called this "heart-space of the Atman" the Brahmarandhra, and the sahasrara chakra, the thousand petalled lotus; for him, these were all the same. They all refer to that secret point in the head where the light of consciousness shines in its purest form. When an individual's kundalini energy is completely roused, it merges into this place in the head. The awakening that occurs in our understanding at that time reveals our complete and total unity in the Divine. When we realize we are in God and God is in us, then there is nothing outside of us. All knowledge is accessible from within.

Sutra 6 The three primary gunas are *sattva, rajas,* and *tamas.* Collectively, they are *Prakriti*, cosmic Nature, the "stuff" of all manifestation. They are simply three different forms of manifestation: still, dynamic, and dense. Sattva guna is pure space, pure light, pure peace. Tamas guna is the opposite, it is density, darkness, and inertia, while rajas guna is fire and dynamic activity. They are at once hierarchical and not hierarchical, since the peace exists in everyone, everyone has dynamic capability, and there is also inertia in everyone. It is just another way of speaking about the spectrum of manifestation. Tamas guna (inertia, thickness) is one end of the spectrum, sattva guna (pure light) is the opposite end, and rajas guna is the meeting of the two, for when pure light and pure density meet, the result is fire. Yet upon reaching sattva guna, there is no more hierarchy. In the pure state of sattva guna, everything is seen as equal; there is no separate mind, no chakras, no nadis—nothing is separate. Sattva guna is pure and perfect balance.

In man, these gunas are found in a state of instability. Sattva causes moments of inspiration, meditative calm, quiet joy, and disinterested affection. Rajas brings out constructive activity, energy, enthusiasm, and physical courage as well as ambition and rage. Tamas is associated with the lowest qualities such as sloth, stupidity, helpless despair, obstinancy and the like.

Sutra 13 The source of liberation is pure consciousness, the awareness of our real Self. The linga in the head is the seat of this pure consciousness. The linga is a stone symbol in the shape of an egg which is the iconography for Shiva as Absolute Potential. It is egg-shaped to represent the unity of the universe—its internal consistency and its formless presence in all directions. Thus, the linga has no corners or edges; it is all OM. It has no face because pure consciousness has no face. The linga in the head corresponds to the *medulla oblongata*, or brain stem, at the junction between brain and spinal column. This is the still point in the head, the place where the ida, pingala, and sushumna meet. For Nityananda, the Shiva linga, the Brahmarandhra, the prana linga, the sahasrara are all the same: the Abode of Shiva, the doorway to God.

Sutra 14 The cities of Kashi and Haridwar were both popular places of pilgrimage for devout Hindus wishing to be freed of sin, but Nityananda asserts that the only truly effective pilgrimage is the inner journey. The nine gates of Haridwar refer to the chakras, while the yajna is the awakening of the inner fire of kundalini which brings the experience of supreme happiness.

Sutra 15 The distinction between manas and buddhi is often made in the Sutras. The terms have very precise technical meanings (see Glossary), but often in the Sutras, a broader meaning is implied. Here, manas refers to the gross expression of the mind through thoughts, concepts, and feelings. This aspect of what we call our mind is limited in every way, and it always gets us into trouble by thinking we want this, we want that, we want something else. Manas reaches for pleasure and seeks to avoid pain. Buddhi, on the other hand, is intelligence. It is farsighted, it is not concerned about either pleasure or pain but rather is only concerned about truth. In the face of every difficulty and complexity, buddhi manifests our own and everyone else's highest best interest. Nityananda called this intelligence subtle discrimination and spiritual discernment.

Nityananda was fond of the railway and often used railroad analogies in his talks. During the twenties and thirties, he spent considerable time traveling by train between Mangalore and Kanhangad, often riding in the engine car; as the engineers came to know him, it became the custom for trains to whistle when passing the Kanhangad Ashram.

Sutra 16 Shiva-Shakti is pure consciousness, the union of pure potential and pure energy that forms the dynamic stillness at the heart of the universe. Kundalini and prana are components of this highest of forces, related to the Shiva-Shakti like body and arm relate to the pure consciousness of being.

Sutra 17 Nadis are the channels of creative energy, of conscious energy. Within the Self, the vibration of Omkar interacts with itself and gives rise to different currents, just as the constant movement of the ocean interacts with variances in depth and temperature to give rise to the currents that flow within it. The currents, though individual, are still water, they are not different in essence from the ocean itself. Our physical being can be compared to a current in the ocean of Omkar, and the nadis are the channels for the flow of this conscious energy that is the essence of the mind, the emotions, and the physical body. The nadis *are* the subtle body. And it is awareness of these nadis that leads us to the recognition of our true nature: the Self.

As Nityananda describes, there are three major nadis. The conscious, creative energy of life itself flows unceasingly through these channels. These nadis are associated with colors as well as with celestial bodies, as listed in the sutra.

Sutra 18 In accordance with the highest and most secret sacred texts, Nityananda distinguishes between the chakra systems above the neck and below the neck, relating them to hatha yoga and raja yoga respectively. For him, hatha yoga and the chakras below the neck relate to the body and the mind, the material world and its attainments. They represent duality, accomplishment, and effort.

To Nityananda, raja yoga is no effort, it is non-dual and indivisible. Thus, the chakras above the neck refer not only to the psychic mechanism but more importantly to the experience of pure, endless, spacious consciousness; consciousness that is unlimited in any way. Raja yoga is the continuous, unbroken awareness of the Absolute.

Sutra 20 Scholars differ about the correct translation of "shunya." While the common translation is "nothingness" or "void," some prefer the precision of "the absence of subject-object relation." In either case, it is simply another word, usually associated with Buddhism, to describe the superconscious state.

Sutra 36 To illustrate the point that for one who sees the Atman "actions are like inaction," a story is told of the great sage Vyasa, who is credited with recording the 18 *Puranas* and the *Mahabharata,* as well as editing the *Vedas*. Early one evening, Vyasa was sitting on the banks of the river Jumna, watching its swirling rise to the high water mark. He was approached by an anxious group of milkmaids, who could find no way to cross the turbulent river. They recognized Vyasa as a great sage and asked that he petition the river to let them cross. The sage asked if they had anything in their pots. They offered him all the curds they had, and he ate all that they offered. Then he stood up and spoke to the river: "If I have not eaten anything, make a passage for these milkmaids." The river responded immediately. Since they had watched Vyasa eat, the milkmaids were totally baffled, until they realized that it was merely the outer body that had eaten. The true Vyasa was identified with the Atman all the while and was not affected.

Sutra 38 The *Ramayana* is a Hindu epic that incorporates history, mythology and spiritual philosophy. It is very popular throughout India; in many villages the re-enactment of its stories continues to be a major yearly event. Thus, the characters and symbolism of the epic are familiar to Indians, educated and rural alike.

The epic is used as allegory here. Just as Sita married Rama and was ever with him, so the mind must be constantly absorbed in the Self. Just as the faithful Lakshmana remained with Rama and Sita in thought and deed, so also the devotee must long always for union with the Self. The ten senses (five of perception and five of action) are Ravana's ten faces. The mind (Sita) is seduced away from the Self (Rama) by the ten senses (Ravana) and held captive. Sita has to be rescued by Lakshmana (standing for *shraddha* [intense faith and constant attention]) and by Hanuman (representing intense devotion and also pranayama which mutually act and react on each other). Krishna is also a name of god, refering to cosmic consciousness.

Sutra 39 The vitality of Life itself is like a resonance that has many chords in it, chords that interact with each other to give rise to all appearances and forms, to the whole material universe. At its essence, these chords are nothing but vibration, sound, mantra. In the universe, the supreme conscious energy of God, as the Supreme Word (*Paravac*) is the Supreme Mantra: the source of all mantra and of all manifestation. In the individual, the natural pulsation of the physical breath and the natural pulsation of the subtle breath (prana) is mantra.

Sutra 42 When you raise desire to its highest level, that is, if you focus desire on the Divine, then you automatically cultivate love and devotion, and subsequently gain release from the pain and suffering of the cycles of birth, death, and rebirth. It is a conscious process. When your energy is scattered about in the form of many different desires, little can be accomplished. Weave together all these small, petty desires and bind them into one very high, powerful desire to see God. This convergence of energy requires that you be filled with love and devotion; you can't hold it all together without love and devotion. Then that love and devotion will slowly reveal to you the vision of the Lord. Love and devotion are totally important.

That is why I would say the most important thing in spiritual growth is the connection between you and the Divine. It is never one thing or the other, it is always what is in the middle. That is true one hundred percent of the time. If you ask is it this or is it that, is it samsara or is it liberation, the answer is always: "Neither." It is what is in the middle.

Sutra 45 In the combined deity Hari-Hara, Hari is Vishnu and Hara is Shiva (in their aspects as part of the Hindu trinity). This god-pair therefore is being used by Nityananda in a special, more limited context. In this sutra, Hari can be taken to mean force, or chit-shakti (mind-energy), that must be dissolved in its source (Hara) in order to reach the One (Paramashiva).

Sutra 49 According to the *Upanishads*, the three states are waking, dream, and deep sleep, yet in this sutra Nityananda lists sleep as the first state. The reference is to being asleep to the soul. That is, we may be constitutionally awake, but if we are not aware of our real Self, we are spiritually asleep. Hence the exhortation in the *Katha Upanishad*: "Arise, awake and stop not till the goal is reached."

In the state of "no mind," sensations, ideas, and time have ceased. The jnani is described in the *Bhagavad Gita* as having his mind dead to the touch of the external and alive to the bliss of the eternal Absolute. To see all things equally is to see the Self in all things and all things within the Self; to be able to see the common factor, the soul or essence, through the multiplicity of forms.

> The recollected mind is awake
> In the knowledge of the Atman,
> which is dark night to the ignorant.
> The ignorant are awake in their sense-life
> which they think is day-light;
> To the seer it is darkness.
>
> *Bhagavad Gita*

Being always "awake in the knowledge of the Atman," the jnani is not affected by the phenomenal sunrise and sunset.

Sutra 53 Once the Self is realized there is no other knowledge to be gained. The *Katha Upanishad* calls this the "knowledge by knowing which all else is known."

The truth of this statement was manifested by Nityananda time after time. He could casually describe a scene from ancient scriptures as if it were taking place right now, or a scene currently happening anywhere in the world as though it were unfolding right before him. In 1940, when Hitler was surging through Europe, someone asked him who would win the war. He replied that Shakti (then held to be represented by Britain) would win in the end. He described Hitler as a great destructive force capable of causing even greater damage, were it not for his lack of faith in the Divine. This lack of faith, Nityananda would say, was the chink in Hitler's armor that would lead to his delusion and destruction. Commenting on Churchill's capability, he used the analogy of the coconut to define his brain power, by saying that his "kernel" was very thick. As described in *Nityananda: The Divine Presence*, even Nityananda's offhand opinions on personalities like Mountbatten and Gandhi, and on world events like India's Independence, always proved correct.

Sutra 79 Nityananda was considered eccentric and even mad in his early days in South Kanara, particularly by the educated and by officials. Whether this aphorism refers to such comments is not known. However, many great mystics have been treated as mad by their contemporaries. For them, on the other hand, absorbed as they are in eternity, all appears the same, mad or clever, sinner or saint. (See also Sutra 31)

Sutra 85 Quieting the tongue is not the real silence; real silence consists of stilling all thought and immersing the mind in Self-knowledge. Concentrating the mind in the sushumna, at the meeting place of the ida and pingala nadis, is the correct practice of silence. It is only through such silence that one can practice yoga and obtain results.

Sutra 96 The "six enemies" are: anger, desire, envy, passion, greed, and delusion.

Sutra 102 Nityananda says that the guru who initiates an aspirant is the "guru of cause," elsewhere called the secondary guru. He is differentiating between the physical teacher, who can *show* the seeker the road to Self-realization, and the "guru of action," who actually walks that road. This action guru, also called the primary guru, resides within the individual, for it is nothing other than the Self of all.

Sutra 141 Nityananda used to say that the three K's were the real obstructions (*upadhis*) on the way to perfection. In Kanarese, these K's were *kanaka*, gold or greed; *kaanta*, women or lust; and *keerti*, desire for name and fame. He used to say that these were obstructions in ascending order, becoming both more subtle and more difficult to overcome. Many, he said, would overcome the first two only to be tripped up by the desire for recognition and fame.

Sutra 152 Kashi is one of the ancient names for the city of Benares, also called Varanasi. Kashi means "City of Light" and so, "City of Shiva." It is one of the most holy cities in India; it is said that one who dies in Benares is freed from the cycle of birth and rebirth.

The suffix "puri" means "abode" and hence village or city.

To reach Benares, you board a train that proceeds steadily towards that destination. To reach the state of chidakash (pure and unbounded awareness), also proceed steadily, by regular practice aimed toward your goal.

Sutra 156 Creative energy, Shakti, the essential knowledge: these are freely available to everyone.

Nityananda often spoke against the rigidities of the caste system. These rigidities, however, have produced some amazing compensations. One famous story concerns the great saint Kanakadasa, who was not permitted into the Krishna temple at Udipi because of his low birth. Few recognized the spiritual greatness of the saint and judged him only by his outer appearance and by the low caste to which his body belonged. Since he was not allowed to enter the shrine, the saint went around to the rear of the temple to pray, peering through a small peephole in the compound wall to catch a glimpse of the statue within. In response to Kanakadasa's sincere devotion, the statue turned 180 degrees to oblige the saint! Even to this day, the temple faces east while the statue faces west.

Sutra 157 Nityananda never referred to himself in the first person, instead he would say "this one" or "this place."

Sutra 163 Prana is the life-force, the vital air, which is a manifestation of the supreme consciousness. Vedanta is here used as "end of knowledge" or "fullness of knowledge."

From the ancient Hindu *Rig Veda* through the Christian *Gospel According to St. John* there has been an emphasis on the Word and an identification of the Word with God. The ancient *rishis* studied carefully the effect of sound on the chakras. As a result of their investigations into the potencies of sound and the human voice, they also discovered that the sound "OM" vibrates throughout the cosmos. Sanskrit therefore was formulated as an essentially phonetic language, with its fifty characters having a vibratory correspondence with the fifty mystic "petals" of the chakras.

Sutra 171 "Those who do not breathe through the mouth or nostrils" are those people who have the awareness of the body as an extension of the highest creative energy of the Self. People think that consciousness arises because of and out of the body, but the reverse is true: the body arises from consciousness. The gross, physical breath is a simple manifestation of the dynamic pulsation of the creative force that is the breath of life in all.

Nityananda's use of the term "swaragya" is interesting because of its political ramifications; it was a popular term during India's struggle for independence in the 1940s. His easy familiarity with both the term and its connotations confirms that Nityananda was quite aware of the external situation.

Sutra 172 To renounce delusion requires renouncing grief and suffering as well. In the final analysis, renouncing delusion means giving up the selfishness of "me" and "mine." It is said that the ant would rather die on a heap of sugar than leave it, and the moth will burn in the fire of the light rather than fly into the dark and survive. An advanced yogi who had been very wealthy at the time of renunciation was praised by his disciples in later years for the greatness of his renunciation of so much wealth. The yogi answered that it was the worldly who were the real renunciates and not he, for they had renounced the whole (God) for the part (world), whereas he had renounced the part for the whole.

Sutra 189 When the mind is merged in the Self, the result is the experience of bliss. As the individual soul becomes fully conscious of the Absolute from which it is evolved, the perfection and fullness of all is experienced:

> OM. That is perfect. This is perfect.
> From the perfect springs the perfect.
> If the perfect is taken from the perfect,
> only the perfect remains.
>
> *Upanishads*

Glossary and Index

Glossary

These definitions are limited to the specific context of this book and do not claim to be authoritative. Sanskrit scholars will find certain transliteration inconsistencies, most notably in the use of the final "a," as in "akash/a." Usage in this volume varies, since reproductions of Nityananda's speech have typically reproduced the dropped-vowel spoken form.

agni   fire; one of the five gross elements of the physical world: earth, water, fire, air and ether or akasha.

ajna chakra   a major chakra, located between the eyebrows in the subtle body; symbolized as two-petaled lotus.

akash/a   lit., the sky; (1) symbol of pure consciousness, also translated as the sky or the infinite; (2) the subtlest of the five elements into which all elements are ultimately resolved, ether.

anahata   (1) anahata chakra is the heart chakra; (2) anahata shabda is the sound of OM heard when the kundalini has risen to the heart chakra; the unstruck sound.

ananda   transcendent bliss, spiritual ecstasy, delight; the essential principle of joy unaffected by worldly objects.

Arjuna   hero of the *Mahabharata*; the teaching of the *Bhagavad Gita* was given to him by Krishna.

Atman   the Self; spirit; eternal principle present in the heart of every living being. See also **jivatman** and **paramatman**.

atmananda   the perfect joy of the Self.

asana   posture or seat.

avadhut/a   a great mystic-renunciate who has risen above body-consciousness, duality, and conventional standards. The avadhut is described in the *Bhagavatam* as one who is free from the consciousness of the ego, roaming free like a child over the face of the earth.

bandh   from "bandhana" meaning "bondage," colloquially used to mean "shut down," as in general strike.

Benares (also Banares and Banaras) Now most often called by its ancient name of Varanasi, because here the two rivers Varuna and Asi meet, the city's other ancient name is Kashi, meaning City of Light or City of Shiva. It is a very holy place for Hindus, for it is thought that to die in Benares, to be burned on its sacred cremation ghats and to have one's ashes scattered into the holy Ganges river puts an immediate end to the cycles of birth and rebirth; thus, liberation.

Bhagavad Gita lit., "Song of the Lord"; part of the epic *Mahabharata*, it contains a systematic statement of the perennial philosophy in the form of a dialogue between Krishna (the incarnation of the god Vishnu) and Arjuna, his chosen devotee.

Bhagavan godhead; one who is full of light.

bhakti ardent devotion and love of God.

bhavana feeling, emotion, sensitivity; creative contemplation.

bindu compact mass of Shakti gathered into an undifferentiated point ready to create.

Brahma one god among many gods, Brahma is the creative spirit of the Hindu trinity, along with Vishnu (preserving, protecting) and Shiva* (dissolving, transforming).
*However, in the form of Paramashiva, Shiva stands for the Absolute, God.

Brahman the Absolute, pure foundational consciousness, the highest reality, the One.

brahmachari one who practices brahmacharya.

brahmacharya the first stage of life; a period of moral education during which celibacy is an important discipline.

brahmaloka loka : region, place; one of the higher planes of existence; the world of Brahma.

Brahmanadi the sushumna.

Brahmarandhra the sahasrara chakra at the top of the head. See also **chidakash/a**.

brahmin a member of the first of four orders of traditional Indian society. This order includes priests and intellectuals.

buddhi (1) a category of the universe; (2) a faculty higher than **manas** (mind); it is the capacity or faculty of discrimination, ascertainment, decision, and will; intelligent will. In considering buddhi, **chitta**, and **manas**, it is important to note the difference between Eastern and Western interpretations of "mind." Eastern thinkers distinguish more finely between mental faculties. See **chitta** for detailed discussion.
In the Sutras, buddhi is used interchangeably with "subtle discrimination," "spiritual discernment," "the steady mind," "higher mind," "wisdom" and the like.

chakra lit., wheel, circle; name given to the centers of conscious energy in the subtle body.
Most scriptures cite seven of these centers, although in the Sutras, Nityananda alludes to a more numerous and complex system. The chakras are associated with the sushumna nadi and flanked on the left and right by the ida and pingala nadis. These nerves and centers are not biological. When the kundalini is awakened, it travels up the sushumna, passing through the chakras. Consciousness widens as each higher chakra is crossed, until the final goal is reached when the kundalini energy merges with its source, the energy of life itself, in the Brahmarandhra.

chidakash/a chit* : absolute consciousness, akash/a : subtle inner space; thus "sky of consciousness."
In the Sutras, also synonymous with: sky of the heart, heart-sky, heart-space, akasha. See also: Brahmarandhra, sahasrara chakra, prana linga, Shiva linga, abode of Shiva, still point, thousand-petalled lotus, Brahmaloka.
*In Sanskrit, the root "chit" becomes "chid" when followed by "akasha."

chit Absolute Consciousness.

chitta individual consciousness, the mind of the empirical individual that is composed of three elements: *buddhi*: the ascertaining intelligence; it gives name and meaning to the perceptions of manas; *ahamkar*: the I-consciousness, the power of self-appropriation, ego; *manas*: the perceiving intelligence, with the senses, builds up perceptions and images, limited mind.
In the Sutras, as in general English usage, "mind" is often used as a synonym for both "chitta" as well as the more limited "manas."

dandi from "danda" meaning "staff"; thus, one who has a staff. A particular order of sannyasis, one of the 10 orders of monks organized by Shankara, are known as the dandi swamis and are identified by the staff they carry.

darshan lit., seeing; (1) the act of seeing the Divinity within the guru or within the representation of the Divine as in a sculpture or painting; (2) a system of philosophy.

dharana lit., holding; holding an object in attention or consciousness, perfect concentration of the mind.

dharma lit., that which holds; moral principle, "that which is decreed" by scripture as duty; Law.

dhyana meditation; an unbroken flow of thought toward the object of concentration. This unbroken flow is the goal of the practice of dharana.

Gita see *Bhagavad Gita*.
Gopala the form of Krishna as the cow-tender.
Govinda lit., giver of enlightenment; a name of Krishna.
Gujarat province on the northwest coast of India, north of Bombay.
guna (1) the three primary constituent gunas of Prakriti are **tamas** (inertia), **rajas** (passion, activity), and **sattva** (balance, light, illumination); (2) quality, property, or attribute.
guru a channel or medium of the grace-bestowing power of God, a perfected spiritual master who has realized identity with the Divine and who can impart this experience to a disciple; the teacher.

Hara a god; one name of Shiva; means one who has conquered himself.
Hari a god; one name of Vishnu or his incarnations (like Krishna); Hari literally means "one who steals," in this context, one who steals the hearts of the devotees.
harijan hari : god, jan : people, so "people of god," the term was popularized by Gandhi in his attempt to improve the lot of the out-castes.
hatha yoga method of obtaining salvation employing vital energy flowing through the nadis; in this yoga, great importance is given to physical fitness; supernormal powers are obtained as a result of the practice of this yoga.
heart-space see **hridayakasha**.
hridaya lit., heart; the mystic center.
hridayakasha hridaya : heart; akasha : space; translated as "sky of the heart," "heart-space," and the like.
In the Sutras, synonymous with the Brahmarandhra, the place in the head where ida, pingala, and sushumna merge, where kundalini is one with the Atman.

ida one of the three primary nadis or channels for the flow of life-energy; the ida begins on the left and with its counterpart the pingala criss-crosses over the central sushumna. All three join and culminate in the Brahmarandhra or the sahasrara chakra. See also **nadi**.

japa devotional exercise consisting in the repetition of a mantra or the name of a deity.

199

jiva   see **jivatman**.
jivatman   individual (Self incarnated in a body).
jivanmukti   jivan : while alive, mukti : liberation; liberation while alive.
jnana   spiritual wisdom.
jnanamrita   the nectar of spiritual wisdom.
jnani   lit., person of spiritual wisdom; one who has realized the Self.

Kanakadasa   a saint belonging to a low caste and refused admission to the Krishna temple in Udipi by the high caste brahmins. He therefore went to the rear of the temple wall to have a peep through an aperture; the Krishna image turned 180 degrees to give him darshan. Even to this day, while the temple faces east (as temples normally do), the image faces west.
karma   (1) act, work, action; according to Hindu philosophical thought, every action performed with desire for its fruit produces an effect and leaves behind a residue which imprisons the soul in the world of existence; (2) law of causation governing action and its effects; moral law.
Kashi   See **Benares**.
kumbhak/a   retention of breath.
kumkum   vermilion powder used in rituals.
kundalini   lit., coiled up; the creative power of Shiva, that aspect of Shakti that lies coiled in three and a half folds in muladhara chakra at the base of the spine.
This Shakti can be awakened by a guru through the process of shaktipat. The main aim of spiritual practice is to rouse this power in man and pass it through the chakras in the sushumna nadi. The seventh chakra is the sahasrara; for the kundalini to reach this point is the highest goal.

linga/m   lit., a sign; (1) as the symbol of Shiva it is revered in the form of a stone post or egg in Shaivite temples or shrines; it is a symbol of Shiva's formless form; (2) the subtle space containing the whole universe in the process of formation and dissolution.

maha   great, high.
Mahabharata   ancient Hindu epic collection; contains eighteen books, including the *Bhagavad Gita*.
mahatma/n   great Self or great soul, realized soul.
mahasamadhi   lit., great resolution, great resolving; when speaking of a saint, it is the conscious shedding of the physical body.
mahashanti   the great peace; the highest peace, peace that passes all understanding.
manas   limited mind; that mental faculty which coordinates the work of the senses, bringing images and perceptions back to the subtle body (it is then the function of **buddhi** to discriminate among the images and ascertain their meaning). See also **chitta**.
mantra   sacred word or formula to be chanted; formulated to awaken the spiritual energy by constant repetition. A japa is normally given by a guru to the disciple to suit his predisposition.
maya   lit., that which measures; (1) the power that measures or limits; (2) the cosmic process or limiting force of the Infinite responsible for the sense of duality.
mind   in the Sutras, used both as synonym for **chitta**, the entire, three-component mental apparatus, and as synonym for **manas**, limited mind.
moksha   liberation.
mouna   silence; vow of silence.
mukti   liberation.
muladhara   chakra located at the base of the spine.

nadi the channels through which conscious creative energy and prana (vital breath) circulate in the subtle body.
nidra sleep, as in: tamo-nidra (gross sleep) or yoga-nidra (subtle state).
nijananda nija : one's own, ananda : bliss; bliss of one's own Self.
nirguna nir : without, guna : quality; without quality, feature, or attribute.
nirvikalpa a state of consciousness free of all thought-constructs.
nityananda eternal bliss.

OM sacred syllable that is Brahman itself as sound; the ultimate, primeval sound.
Omkar kar : from the root *kri*, to do; thus the sound or power of OM.

para the highest; the Absolute (usually seen as a prefix).
parabrahma the Absolute; God.
paramahamsa lit., supreme swan; the mythical swan Hamsa is reputed to have been capable of drawing milk out of a mixture of milk and water. A paramahamsa is therefore a realized person who can distinguish real from unreal.
paramananda bliss of the highest, bliss of the Absolute.
Paramatman lit., Supreme Self; synonymous with Atman.
Parvati goddess; consort of Shiva (Shiva here refers to one god of Hindu trinity).
pingala one of the three principal nadis.
Prakriti unconscious cosmic Nature; the energy that evolves as the world.
prana (1) that force which animates, vital air, the universal life-force; (2) in the human organism, prana has five functions, the first of which, the out-breath, is also called prana. Prana as life-force is the natural connecting link between consciousness and its physical manifestations.
prana linga the spiritual form of Shiva the Absolute.
pranava resonance; used to designate the syllable OM; the universal sound.
prana-shakti the divine Shakti working both in the universe and in the individual (in the individual, kundalini is the form or expression of this Shakti).
prana vayu the breath of life; the life-force or energy.
prema devotional love.
puja worship or ritual.
puraka the inhaled breath.
Puranas lit., ancient; a collection of symbolical and allegorical writings, mythological in character; there are eighteen such scriptures.
puri lit., abode; hence, as suffix denotes city or village, as in Ganeshpuri: "abode or village of Ganesha."
purna perfect; full of divine consciousness.
Purusha (1) the Self, pure conscious being; (2) in Sankya philosophy, Spirit in contradistinction to Prakriti, cosmic Nature (unconscious energy from which the world evolves); (3) in literary Sanskrit, commonly rendered "man."

raja yoga lit., the king of yogas; emphasizes mental and spiritual discipline rather than physical culture.
In the Sutras, Nityananda uses raja yoga to denote the highest yoga; that which is non-dual and indivisible—the continuous, unbroken awareness of the Self.
rajas one of the three primary gunas; the principle of motion, activity, passion, and pain.
Ramayana great epic of Hindu literature; along with the *Puranas* and the later epic *Mahabharata*, it forms the foundation of Indian historical writing. It tells the story of Rama and Sita; according to the scriptures, Rama is the 7th incarnation of Vishnu, and Sita is his divine consort. The *Ramayana* tells of the abduction of Sita by

the 10-headed Ravana, a powerful, evil king of Sri Lanka, and her subsequent rescue. In the fight with Ravana, Rama is helped by Hanuman (subsequently venerated as a great devotee) and by Rama's brother Lakshmana.

rechaka   the exhaled breath.

Rig Veda   first and most ancient of four *Vedas*, perhaps dating from as early as 1000 B.C. (dates disputed).

rishi   lit., seer; wise man or sage; the hymns of the *Vedas* are said to have been revealed to the rishis of ancient India.

sadhana   pursuit of an ideal; the practice of spiritual discipline.

sadhu   lit., good, holy; a holy man.

sahasrar/a   lit., thousand; highest chakra of the subtle body, symbolized by a thousand-petalled lotus or a thousand-spoked wheel; where kundalini unites with Shiva; seat of pure consciousness.

samadhi   lit., resolution, resolving; "drawing together of the mind"; extraordinary state in which the fluctuations of the mind are stilled; superconscious state. There are two types of samadhi: *sa-vikalpa* in which distinction between subject and object is retained, and *nir-vikalpa* in which the yogi realizes his total one-ness (union) with the Absolute.

samsara   lit., movement; existence in the phenomenal world of contradictions and dualities.

sannyasa   renunciation.

sannyasi   lit., one who casts away, renounces; one who has renounced worldly bonds in order to devote him/herself to the spiritual life.

sat-chit-ananda   being-consciousness-bliss; the three-fold description of Brahman, the Absolute: *sat* : the essence of existence, "be-ness"; *chit* : consciousness; and *ananda* : bliss, joy, ecstasy.

sattva   one of the three primary gunas; the principle of being, light, happiness and harmony; essence; balance.

Self   self-existent, pure awareness and pure consciousness, self-luminous, and according to some schools of philosophy, also self-conscious; only one Self is manifested in all minds and bodies.
In the Sutras, synonymous with Atman, and thus with the Absolute, etc.

shabda   sound.

Shakti   power; active, creative power of the Divine.

shanti   peace.

Shiva   (1) the Absolute; pure consciousness, the transcendent divine principle; (2) one of the gods of the Hindu trinity, along with Vishnu and Brahma.

shraddha   intense faith, deeper than mind; involves both knowledge and will or dynamism; it is also held to indicate a pleasant inclination towards yoga.

shuddha bhavana   shuddha : pure; bhavana : feeling, thought, contemplation.

shudra   one belonging to the fourth order of the traditional Indian society.

siddhi   lit., accomplishment, achievement; power attained through yogic practice.

shunya   (Buddhism): the void, emptiness; state in which no object is experienced.

sushumna   one of the primary nadis; the middle or central channel for the flow of the life-energy.

sushupti   state of deep, dreamless sleep; one of man's four states of consciousness: *jagrat* : waking, *svapna* : dreaming, *sushupti* : deep sleep, and *turiya* : the fourth, the Atman.

swami   lit., master of one's Self; title given to monks and religious heads of Maths (temples).

swarajya lit., kingdom of the Self, hence an attribute of Atman implying perfect freedom. In the political sense it means freedom from foreign rule, and so self-government.

tamo-nidra state of gross sleep.

tamas one of the three primary gunas; principle or quality of inertia, insensitivity, and delusion.

tapas lit., heat.

tapasya lit., that which generates heat or energy; brooding, incubation; the concentration of energy to generate creative force.

tattva "thatness," the very being of a thing; principle or category.

turiya lit., the fourth; the fourth state of consciousness beyond the states of waking, dreaming, and deep sleep and stringing together all the states; the transcendental Self.

upadhi limiting adjunct or condition; obstacle.

upanayana initiation ceremony undergone by all young high-caste Hindu males at about the age of seven before going to the guru for education.

vairagya (1) intense dispassion for worldliness, not colored by desire; (2) desirelessness; (3) renunciation.

vasana lit., smell; impregation, residual trace left by any act; tendency, habit energy; generally applied to indicate tendency, predisposition or latency at birth as a result of character and action in previous incarnations.

vayu (1) air, the fourth element; (2) the vital air, the breath of life, the life force: prana.

Veda from the root "vid" meaning "to know," "veda" literally means "wisdom." The *Vedas*, edited by the great Vyasa, constitute the knowledge of God revealed to seers at the beginning of each cycle. There are four *Vedas*: *Rig, Yajur, Sama,* and *Atharva*. Each is divided into four parts: Samhita (hymns), Brahmana (rituals), Aranyaka (to be read in retirement in forest after fulfilling worldly responsibilities - aranya is forest) and Upanishad (lit., "sit near;" , that is, sit near the guru).

Vedanta lit., the end or goal of the *Vedas* (anta : end); a system of philosophy based on the *Vedas*.
Nityananda uses both of these terms, *Veda* and *Vedanta*, to indicate philosophical scholarship in general.

vibhuti (1) lit., force of God used to manifest extraordinary people or things in which this force manifests; (2) any object so manifested; (3) ash (by derivation, since ash has often been the object miraculously manifested).

vishva-prana lit., universal energy.

yajna Vedic ritual; sacrifice or fire ceremony.

yantra symbolic drawing or visual contemplative device; the yantra represents the cosmos and is often used as an aid to concentration.

yoga In the Sutras, the science through which individuals recognize their essential identity with God; awareness, transformation of human consciousness into divine consciousness.

yoga-nidra subtle sleep, sleep of awareness.

yogi lit., united; one who studies and practices yoga, who is absorbed in spiritual practices with the sole intent of uniting the individual with the universal.

yukti reason, argument, cleverness, skill.

INDEX

abode of Shiva, 20, 185. *See also* Brahmarandhra
Absolute
    synonyms for, 14
acharya, 129
Achutamama, 73, 101
agni, 108
ajna chakra, 19, 50
akasha, 42, 63, 65, 112, 129, 151. *See also* chidakash(a)
ananda, 55, 179
asana, 144
ashram, 8, 186
atma-bindu, 64
Atman, 31-68
    is the Self, 15
    synonyms for, 14
avadhut, 129-131
    Nityananda as, 11

bandh, 122
Benares, 6, 192
Bhagavad Gita, 189, 190
bhakta(s), 119
bhakti, 51, 57, 137, 139, 154. *See also* devotion
Bhimeswari Temple, 8
bindu, 42, 50, 139
    Omkar and, 104
body-idea, 128, 159. *See also* ego
Bombay, 8, 122
bondage, 23, 60, 88, 105, 107
Brahma, 128

brahmachari, 132
Brahmaloka, 167
Brahman, 183
Brahmanadi. *See* sushumna
Brahmananda, 68, 97, 108, 167
Brahmanandapuri, 158
Brahmarandhra, 43, 44, 57, 91, 162, 184, 185
    as mantra, 64
    breath and, 57, 169
    kundalini and, 25
    nadis and, 96
    prana and, 54
    Shiva and, 149
    synonyms for, 20, 65
brahmin, 67, 154, 159, 160, 165
breath, 59, 85, 107, 166
    internal, 165, 174
    OM-sound and, 163
    regulating the, 53, 66, 167, 169
breath of life, 17, 90, 162. *See also* prana
Britain, 190
buddhi, 41, 44, 71-99, 81, 136, 154, 185, 186. *See also* mind; intelligence; discrimination
    as discriminative mind, 23, 24
    breath and, 161
    chidakash and, 65
    dharana and, 90
    in sushumna, 81
    jnana and, 96
    mind and, 94, 124, 162
    path of, 112-115

sattva guna and, 153
the Way of, 48, 156
Buddhism, 187
Buddhist, 12

caduceus, 17
Calicut, 6, 7
camphor, 69, 94, 162
caste system, 192
causal guru, 21, 22
cause and effect, 82, 112, 136, 139, 159
  are one in Self, 106
  bondage of, 25
chaitanyananda, 108
chakra(s), 50, 69, 184, 185, 193
  above the neck, 177
  description of, 17-20
  system of, 47, 187
chapati, 31
chidakash(a), 11, 22, 33, 65, 113, 183, 192. See also hyridayakasha, Brahmarandhra
  as experience of pure consciousness, 20
  no duality in, 21
Chidakash Gita, 183
chid-guna, 88
chit, 179
chit-shakti, 189
chitta, 60, 113
  purification of, 23
chitta kundalini, 16
Churchill, Winston, 190
concentration, 166. See also dharana; meditation
  breath and, 163

dandi, 132
darshan, 11, 119
desirelessness, 131, 138, 151
  faith and, 92
  liberation and, 60, 66
  is supreme joy, 89
detachment, 136
devotion, 135, 138, 140
dharana, 48, 90, 156
dharma, 113
diet, rules for, 176
discernment (spiritual), 186
discrimination (subtle), 59, 81, 178, 186
  search for truth and, 66, 67, 79
  mind and, 93
dynamic stillness, 19, 20. See also Brahmarandhra

ego, 24, 49, 94. See also body-idea
equal sightedness, 24, 39, 56, 61, 140, 151
equal vision, 113, 124, 131
  devotion and, 140

faith, 42, 48, 52, 63, 162, 163
  desire and, 92
fear, 140, 142, 149
fire, 175
  inner, 176
  of yoga, 154

Ganesha, 11
Ganeshpuri, 8-11, 119, 122
Gandhi, Mahatma Mohandas, 190
Gita, 13. See also *Bhagavad Gita*
Gospel of St John, 14, 192
Govinda, 174
grace (of the guru), 56
Gujarat(i), 122
guru, 23, 38, 40, 96, 119, 132, 139, 140, 143, 148. See also teacher
  grace of, 32, 56
  Nityananda's, 7
  merging real with unreal, 87
  of action, 22, 126
  of cause, 126
  physical teacher, 127
  supreme, 64, 128, 143
  two aspects of, 22, 126, 127, 125, 191
  Western attitude toward, 3, 4
guru-kripa, 32
Guruvan, 6, 8, 32
guna(s), 15, 24, 36, 38, 50, 88, 114, 184

Hanuman, 188
Hara, 68
Hari, 68, 96, 149, 154
Hari-Hara, 189
Haridwar, 43, 185
harijan, 6
hatha yoga, 47, 130, 187
heart-space, 20, 21, 33, 37, 151, 158, 166, 184. See also hyridayakasha
heart-sky, 61, 112
Himalayas 6, 7
Hitler, Adolf, 190
hotel bandh, 122
householder, 159, 160
hridayakash(a), 37, 91, 183. See also chidakasha; Brahmarandhra
  as experience, 20

ida, 17, 45, 169, 185, 191
Independence (India's), 190
inner sight, 37, 144
intelligence (subtle), 81, 178
    guru and, 96
    practice and, 151
Ishwar Iyer, 6-8, 12, 74

Japan, 7
jiva, 21, 41, 42, 52, 81, 162, 178
jivanmukti, 35, 44, 53, 129, 131
jivatman, 15, 16, 39, 103, 179, 183
jnana, 23, 78, 96
    Atman perceived by, 61
jnanamrita, 43
jnani, 23, 24, 131, 167, 189, 190
    attention in buddhi, 80
    has no mind, 75
    like the tortoise, 79
    loves all equally, 75

Kaduva, 74
Kanakadasa, 192
Kanarese, 12, 183
Kanhangad, 8, 32, 120, 121, 186
Kanaran, 122
karma, 60, 123, 179
    dissolves in Self, 11
    Self and, 11, 90, 96
Kashi, 43, 158, 173, 185, 192
Katha Upanishad, 189, 190
Kaup, 101
Khoday (Lakshmansa), 119
Kothamangalam, 74
Krishna, 64, 102, 174, 188
    Temple at Udipi, 192
kumbhaka, 57
kumkum, 8
kundalini, 19, 23, 40, 56, 183, 184, 186
    as individual creative energy, 20
    fire of, 23, 185
    sushumna and, 96
    three aspects of, 16
kundalini-shakti, 23-25, 50, 54, 69

Lakshmana, 64, 188
liberation 88, 108, 113, 162, 173, 178, 185
    age no barrier to, 175
    desire and, 131
    detachment and, 136, 148
    mind and, 23, 48, 136
    process of, 21-25
    reach through path of sushumna, 137
    recognition of Self as, 25
    ritual and, 173, 189
    unity as, 34, 49, 66
life-breath, 168
Life-Force, 40. *See also* kundalini; Shakti
linga(m), 8, 43, 185
    in the head, 20

Madras, 37
Mahabharata, 187
mahatma, 3, 61, 76
mahasamadhi, 8, 119
mahashanti, 113
Malayasia, 7
manas, 44, 159, 185, 186
    limited mind, 23, 24
Mangalore, 8, 12, 32, 102, 186
mantra, 14, 25, 26, 50, 64, 125, 165, 174, 188
    breath as, 57
maya, 13, 15, 36, 38, 97, 149, 154, 171
    effort and, 94
meditation 42, 47, 48, 49, 56. *See also* dharana
    experiences in, 171
    role of mind and breath in, 24
medulla oblongata, 185
milkmaids, 187, 188
mind. *See also* buddhi; chitta; manas
    cause of good and evil, 95
    delusion of, 92
    reflection of Self, 36
    root of bondage and liberation, 88
    teacher and, 129
mittha, 136
moksha, 136
mouna, 96
Mountbatten, Louis (Earl of), 190
mukti, 51, 77
muladhara (chakra), 47
    kundalini dormant in, 19

nadi(s), 17, 22, 43, 44, 67, 184, 186, 187
    purifying the, 54, 57
    three major, 45, 96
nijananda, 69
nirguna, 82
nirvana, 184
nirvikalpa, 43
nishkama bhakti, 113
Nityananda
    detachment of, 4
    education of, 12

early years, 6-11
in Ganeshpuri, 8-11,
philosophy of, 13-25
talks from trance, 12
temples dedicated to, 8
travels of, 6, 7
Nityananda: The Divine Presence, 6, 190
nityananda, 108
North Kerala, 8

OM, 113, 128, 139, 185
  breath and, 163
  constitutes the Vedas, 165
  creation and, 103
  pervades all, 112, 171, 193
  yoga and, 162
Omkar, 14-16, 101-115, 141, 159, 186
Omkar-Shakti, 102
OM-sound, 14, 112, 178

Pandalaquin (railway station), 74
Pandavas, 102
Parabrahma, 22, 35, 83
  synonyms for, 14
para kundalini, 16
paramahamsa, 179
paramananda, 66, 108
paramashiva, 22
paramatman, 15, 39, 104, 183
Paravac, 188
pariah, 157, 159
Parvati, 11
peace, 66, 157, 175, 177
  highest state, 112
pingala, 17, 45, 47, 96, 169, 185, 191
Puklun, 120
Prakriti, 15, 184. *See also* guna(s)
prana, 17, 54, 161, 166, 186, 188, 192. *See also*
  breath of life
  disease and, 150
  link between mental/physical, 16
  Vedanta and, 165
prana kundalini, 16
prana linga, 50, 185
pranava, 14, 105, 111, 171
  Omkar and, 107
prana-vayu, 90, 107, 169
pranayama, 17, 47, 167, 188
prema, 135
pundit, 73
puraka, 57
Puranas, 187

Purusha, 107

raja yoga, 47, 52, 53, 130, 144, 187
rajas (guna), 15, 184, 185
Ram (Nityananda as boy), 6
Rama, 64, 174, 188
Ramayana, 188
Rameshwar, 173
Ravana, 64, 188
rechaka, 57
renunciation, 24, 179, 192, 139
  sum of Vedas, 13
Rig Veda, 14, 192
rishi(s), 193
royal road (to liberation), 21, 126, 150, 158
  is within, 31

sad-guna, 88
sadhana, 24, 96, 119-179, 159
  goal of, 11
sadhu, 120
sahasrara (chakra), 24, 50, 184, 185. *See also*
  dynamic stillness; Brahmarandhra
  union of Shiva and Shakti in, 19
Sai Baba of Shirdi, 120
sakkare, 136
samadhi, 42, 53, 80, 184
  equal vision and, 124
same-sightedness, 38, 135, 167. *See also* equal
  vision
samsara, 66, 189
sannyasa, 129
sannyasi, 24, 34, 129, 166, 179
  Brahmnarandhra and, 91
  desire and, 95
  Nityananda as, 11
Sanskrit, 24, 193
Sat, 179
sat-chit-ananda, 14, 25, 49, 66, 108, 113, 133, 171, 179
sattva (guna), 15, 184, 185
  buddhi and, 153
  pure light, 80
Self (synonyms for), 14
Shabda, 14
Shakti, 40, 44, 93, 119, 149, 169. *See also* Shiva;
  Omkar; kundalini
  union of Shiva and, 11, 19, 20, 114
  pure energy, 14
  represented by Britain, 190
  same as Omkar, 16, 111
shaktipat, 19, 23

Shankara, 12
shanti, 158
Shirdi Sai Baba, 120
Shiva, 14, 43, 96, 154, 185, 189
    as the Supreme, 8, 11, 42, 68, 104
    Brahmarandhra and, 149
    one aspect of trinity, 11
    union with Shakti, 19, 20, 114
Shivananda, 7
Shivanandapuri, 158
Shiva linga, 107, 185, 54
Shiva-Shakti, 25, 83, 104, 186. *See also* dynamic stillness
    highest state, 89
    in the Brahmarandhra, 44
    union of individual and Divine in, 25
shraddha, 188
shunya, 48, 184, 187
siddha(i), 51, 65
silence, 191
Singapore, 7, 8
Sita, 64, 188
six enemies, 114, 124, 154, 191
sky of consciousness, 38, 49, 51
sky of the heart, 57, 66
South Kanara, 8, 101, 191
sthana, 31
subtle body, 17, 45
subtle discrimination. *See* discrimination (subtle)
subtle intelligence. *See* intelligence (subtle)
sushumna, 17, 45, 50, 51, 185, 191
    breath and, 167
    liberation and, 137
    nadi of God, 67
    seat of kundalini, 96
sushupti, 56
swami, 87, 132
Swamiji, 120
swarajya, 169, 193

tamas, 15, 184, 185
Tantric, 12
tapas(ya), 125
teacher. *See also* guru
    physical, 22
    universal, 129
ten senses, 64
ten sounds, 43, 45
third eye, 56, 67, 114
"this one", 102, 161, 192

thousand petalled lotus, 78, 184
three humors, 166
three Ks, 191
three states, 41, 113, 189
    not real to jnani, 76, 87
tortoise, 79
turiya, 184

Udipi, 8, 73
Unniamma, 6
untouchable, 132, 157, 160
upadhis, 191
upanayana, 67
Upanishads, 189, 194

Vac, 14
vairagya, 24, 62, 148, 150, 151. *See also* desirelessness; detachment
Varanasi, 192
vasana(s), 115
vayu, 48, 52, 108, 145
    moves in nadis, 44
Veda, 13, 61, 113, 165, 187
Vedanta(ic), 12, 13, 54, 132, 157, 165, 192
vibhuti (ash), 74
Vishnu, 189, 128
vital air, 104. *See also* prana
vivekananda, 108
Vyasa, 187, 188

wisdom-nectar, 92

yajna, 43, 185
yantra, 50
yoga, 49, 108, 148, 162, 191
    as study of Self, 13
    balancing the breath is, 56
    escape from karma, 123
    fire of, 22, 57, 154
    goal of, 19
    practices of, 3, 20
    union with God, 65
yogananda, 66, 179
yoga-nidra, 79
yogi(s), 34, 61, 76, 87, 166, 179, 193
    buddhi and, 96
    desire and, 96
    have no sense of difference, 83
yukti, 44, 93, 139